LEARN SPANISH FAST FOR ADULT BEGINNERS

Learn to Speak Spanish The Fun and Easy Way in Just 30 Days

LEARN SPANISH
GRAMMAR WORKBOOK

CONTENTS

DISCLAIMER NOTICE:

Please note the information contained within this document is for educational and entertainment purposes only.

All effort has been executed to present accurate, up to date, reliable, complete information. No warranties of any kind are declared or implied. Readers acknowledge that the author is not engaged in the rendering of legal, financial, medical or professional advice. The content within this book has been derived from various sources.

Please consult a licensed professional before attempting any techniques outlined in this book.

By reading this document, the reader agrees that under no circumstances is the author responsible for any losses, direct or indirect, that are incurred as a result of the use of the information contained within this document, including, but not limited to, errors, omissions, or inaccuracies.

INTRODUCTION

Eager to learn Spanish but feeling stuck with formal lessons and apps? Losing motivation despite initial excitement? Fear not! Learning a new language requires effort, but the right approach can rekindle your enthusiasm.

Introducing the "Learn Spanish Grammar Workbook for Adult Beginners" – an engaging, effective solution tailored for those tired of feeling overwhelmed. Scheduling lessons becomes enjoyable when the learning process is pleasant and manageable, ensuring you stay motivated.

This workbook breaks the mold with micro-lessons, delivering bite-sized information and loads of practice. From the get-go, our easy-to-follow online workbook captivates you with concise grammar explanations and fun exercises. We recognize your time constraints, avoiding the stress of adding Spanish to an overflowing to-do list. Learning should be a relaxing, enjoyable activity, akin to exercise; pleasurable and effective.

Dive into real-life scenarios, where vocabulary is learned contextually, and grammar is explained within everyday situations. Short stories, scenes, and songs enhance your grasp of the language. Extensive practice reinforces concepts, creating a cumulative learning experience where each class builds on the last.

Our program transforms Spanish into a seamless part of your life. Whether reading, writing, or engaging with various media, you'll gain insights into Spanish-speaking cultures. Hundreds have successfully read and written Spanish within weeks, enhancing travel experiences, job prospects, and cultural appreciation.

Structured classes in the workbook bring a sense of accomplishment. Clear grammatical explanations and relevant exercises propel you forward, boosting confidence. Express your thoughts in Spanish, understand various resources, and read authentic content like poems and social media excerpts.

Focused, short lessons eliminate overwhelm, ensuring steady progress. Each class tackles one grammar issue, building a strong foundation for the next. So why wait? Start now, and unlock a world of possibilities; new friends, exciting trips, and career growth await!

¡Vamos a aprender español! (Let's learn Spanish!) **One final thing before you start**: Find your bonus content immediately before Chapter 1 begins. You can go check it out right now. Enjoy!

We invite you to scan this "QR code"

By using the camera of your phone aiming at the QR code and clicking on the link that appears

to access your bonus content:

SCAN TO CLAIM YOUR BONUSES

OR

ENTER THIS URL IN YOUR WEB BROWSER:

bit.ly/speakspwb

(only use lowercase letters)

SECTION I:
GRAMMAR WORKBOOK

CHAPTER 1:

SUBJECT PRONOUNS
GOOD MORNING AND GOODBYE

First things first! The initial step to learning any language always begins with subject pronouns. In English, these are words like 'I,' 'You,' and 'They.' They indicate *who* exactly we're talking about and they're essential for everyday conversation! Without them, it would be impossible to describe ourselves, other people, and how events have affected us. They are some of the most basic building blocks of any language.

So, let's take a look at what subject pronouns in Spanish are!

1.1 Subject Pronouns

English	Spanish	Pronunciation
I	**yo**	*[io]*
You (informal, singular)	**tú**	*[too]*
You (formal, singular)	**usted**	*[oos-tehd]*
He	**él**	*[ehl]*
She	**ella**	*[eh-yah]*
They (masculine)	**ellos**	*[eh-yohs]*
They (feminine	**ellas**	*[eh-yahs]*
We (masculine)	**nosotros**	*[noh-soh-trohs]*
We (feminine)	**nosotras**	*[noh-soh-trahs]*
You (formal and informal, plural.)	**ustedes**	*[oos-the-des]*
You (inf., plural, masc.)	**vosotros***	*[boh-soh-trohs]*
You (inf., plural, fem.)	**vosotras***	*[boh-soh-trahs]*

* *Vosotros* and *vosotras* are only used in Spain. Although people in other Spanish-speaking countries will understand you, it will come across as unusual to them.

You'll notice that, in Spanish, there are a lot more subject pronouns than in English! Aside from *who* they reference, they're also split up based on:

➲ Formality of the situation.

➲ Genders of the people you're talking about.

➲ Quantity of subjects, i.e., whether you're just talking to or about one person or more.

Unlike English, there are different Spanish pronouns for 'you' and 'they' depending on how many people you're talking to or talking about. Saying *ustedes* **would be like the equivalent of saying 'you all' or 'both of you.'**

Let's get familiar with these pronouns, shall we?

Note on Abbreviations: masculine (m.), feminine (f.), informal (inf.), formal (form.), singular (sing.), plural (pl.)

1.1. Practice

A. Translate the following pronouns:

1. We (f.): _____

2. I: _____

3. They (f.): _____

4. They (m.): _____

5. You (inf. pl. in Spain): _____

6. You (inf. sing.): _____

7. You (f. inf. pl. in Spain & LatAm): _____

8. We (m.): _____

B. Write the correct subject pronoun:

1. _____ voy a tu casa (*I'm going to your house*).

2. _____ somos tus amigos (*we—m.—are your friends*).

3. _____ sois los mejores (*you—m. inf. pl. in Spain—are the best*)

4. _____ son hombres (*you— f. and inf. pl. Spain & LatAm—are men*).

5. _____ son amigos (*they—m.—are friends*).

6. _____ eres mujer (*you—sing. inf. are a woman*).

C.   **Replace the names between parentheses with an adequate pronoun:**

1.   (Pablo) _____ y (María) _____ van a casarse (*will get married*).

2.   (They) _____ van a casarse (*will get married*) en una iglesia (*in a church*).

3.   (You/masculine/plural/informal Spain) _____ estáis invitados a la boda (*are invited to the wedding*).

4.   ¿ _____ (Luisa and you/informal), queréis ir a la boda? (*want to go to the wedding?*)

5.   (Tomás and I) _____ tenemos una sorpresa (*have a surprise*) para (they/masculine) _____.

6.   (Pedro) _____ vive en México (*lives in México*).

7.   (Julia) _____ vive en Ecuador (*lives in Ecuador*).

1.2 The Difference Between Formal (*usted*) and Informal (*tú*) Pronouns

Earlier, we briefly touched on how different pronouns are used based on the formality of a situation. For example, if you were speaking directly to one person ('you'), you'd use the word **tú** in an informal situation and **usted** in a formal situation. But what exactly constitutes an informal or formal situation?

You'd use the formal word **usted** in interactions with people like:

⮌ Your boss

⮌ A stranger or new acquaintance (unless you dislike them and want them to know it!)

⮌ A salesperson

⮌ The cashier at the bank

⮌ Older people

Its abbreviation is **Ud.** (always with a capital **U**).

You'd use the informal pronoun **tú** with:

⮌ Your friends

⮌ Your family

⮌ Children and animals

⮌ People you intend to insult

⮌ Other young people (if you're young, too)

What if you're not sure whether to use *tú* or *usted*?

Situations may arise where you're not sure whether to go with the informal or formal pronoun. In this case, be safe and go with the formal *usted*! It's much better to be overly polite than to risk coming across as rude or insulting

> **Tip: ¿Ustedes or vosotros?**
>
> Remember **vosotros** and **vosotras** from the table of pronouns? It means the exact same thing as **ustedes** but it's not used in the same countries.

In Latin American Spanish, **ustedes** is the plural of both **usted and tú**; that is, **ustedes** is both formal and informal. Every time you address a group of people, whether the relationship is formal or informal, you use **ustedes**. Its abbreviation is **Uds. Vosotros** is not used in Latin America.

In Spain, they use both **ustedes** (formal settings and plural of **tú** and **usted**) and **vosotros** as the plural of **tú.** The form **vosotros** is only used in Spain. The deciding factor is the level of formality you want to express: **vosotros** is informal and **ustedes** is formal.

Basically, you have something like this:

Latin America	**Spain**
Singular - Tú (informal) / Usted (formal)	Singular - Tú (informal) / Usted (formal)
Plural - Ustedes (formal and informal)	Plural - Ustedes (formal) /
Vosotros (not used)	Vosotros (informal)

Tip: The masculine plural form **ellos** refers to a group of males or to a group that includes both males and females. The feminine plural form **ellas** only refers to a group of females. In other words, the default word for 'They' is **ellos**, unless you're referring to a group of people that's entirely female.

Interesting fact: In Spanish, there is no subject pronoun, **it**. You use **él** and **ella** to refer to people, and sometimes animals. You don't use **él** and **ella** to refer to things. It would be like calling a shoe or a potato 'he' and 'she.' Quirky, but not exactly accurate!

Ready to practice words? Let's go!

1.2. Practice

A. **What would you say with each of the following, tú or usted?**

1. Your grandmother _____
2. A co-worker _____
3. A flight attendant _____
4. Your boss _____
5. A little boy _____
6. A professor _____
7. A repair person _____
8. Your cousin _____
9. Your best friend _____
10. Your father-in-law _____

B. **Say which pronoun you would use according to the situation:**

tú / vosotros / ustedes

1. You ask the waiter at a restaurant in Latin America when your table will be ready. He answers: _____ son los siguientes (*you're up next*).

2. You ask your friends in Spain if they want to come with you to the park: ¿ _____ queréis venir conmigo? (*Do you want to come with me?*)

3. You tell your friends in Latin America that they're your best friends: _____ son mis mejores amigos (*You are my best friends*).

4. You tell your coworkers in Spain they are great: _____ sois geniales (*You are great*).

5. You tell your coworkers in Latin America: "You guys are great": _____ son geniales (*You are great*).

6. You tell your friend in Latin America: _____ sabes cocinar muy bien. (*You know how to cook very well*).

1.3 Greetings and Expressions of Politeness

As we mentioned earlier, your word choices will vary depending on the formality of the situation. This applies to pronouns, and it also applies to longer exchanges, like greetings. In English, formality and informality matters too! For example, you probably wouldn't enter a formal meeting with your boss and say, "Hey, what's up?"

In Spanish, it's no different. You'll have different greetings for different types of situations. The words might mean essentially the same thing, but the choices convey whether you're familiar or unfamiliar with the person or people you're addressing.

Informal Greeting

Consider the following informal greeting between Maria and Pedro, two young housemates that go to the same college. Since they're both peers, they'll use informal language with each other, even if they're not that close.

María: Hola, Pedro.
           (Hi, Pedro)

Pedro: Hola, María. ¿Qué tal?
           (Hi, Maria. How's it going?)

María: Bien. ¿Y tú?
           (Good. And you?)

Pedro: ¡Muy bien! Hasta luego.
           (Very good! See you later)

María: Adiós.
           (Bye)

Formal Greeting

Now, let's look at a formal greeting between Señor Pérez and Señorita Alonso. Señor Pérez is a security guard at Señorita Alonso's apartment building. Even though they're both middle-aged, they would use formal language with each other since they don't know each other well and they aren't exactly peers.

Señor Pérez:	Buenas tardes, señorita Alonso.
	(Good afternoon, Señorita Alonso)
Señorita Alonso:	Buenas tardes, señor Pérez. ¿Cómo está?
	(Good afternoon, Señor Pérez. How are you?)
Señor Pérez:	Muy bien, gracias. ¿Y usted?
	(Very good, thank you. And you?)
Señorita Alonso:	Muy bien, gracias. Adiós.
	(Very good, thanks. Goodbye)
Señor Pérez:	Hasta luego.
	(See you later)

Both the informal and formal greetings essentially say the same thing, but they'll use different words in the formal exchange to express politeness. That said, some words and phrases will remain the same. You can still say **bien** or **muy bien** to say you're doing well or very well, and in either situation, you'll still say **adiós** to say goodbye.

Vocabulary: Greetings

English	Spanish	Pronunciation
Hi	**Hola**	*[oh-lah]*
How's it going?	**¿Qué tal?**	*[keh-tahl]*
Good	**Bien**	*[byehn]*
And you?	**¿Y tú?**	*[ee too]*
Very good	**Muy bien**	*[mwee byehn]*
See you later	**Hasta luego**	*[ahs-tah lweh-goh]*
Goodbye	**Adiós**	*[ah-dyohs]*
Bye	**Chau**	*[chow]*

¿Qué tal?, ¿Cómo estás?, and **¿Y tú?** are greeting expressions used in informal situations, with people you know well, on a first-name basis.

> **Tip: Spanish does not use one question mark, but two.** We use an inverted question mark at the beginning of the sentence.

Vocabulary: More Greetings

English	Spanish	Pronunciation
Good morning	Buenos días	[bweh-nohs dee-ahs]
Good afternoon	Buenas tardes	[bweh-nahs tahr-dehs]
Good evening, good night	Buenas noches	[bweh-nahs noh-chehs]
Mr.	Señor (Sr.)	[seh-nyohr]
Mrs.	Señora (Sra.)	[seh-nyoh-rah]
Miss	Señorita (Srita.)	[seh-nyoh-ree-tah]
How are you?	¿Cómo está usted?	[koh-moh ehs-tah oos-tehd]
And you?	¿Y usted?	[ee oos-tehd]
See you later	Hasta luego	[ahs-tah lweh-goh]
See you tomorrow	Hasta mañana	[ahs-tah mah-nyah-nah]

¿Cómo está? and ¿Y usted? are used to address someone with whom you have a more formal relationship, like your boss or a salesperson.

1.4 Language Etiquette

In our daily lives, one of the most important ways we express kindness and courtesy is through our words. And while it may be second nature for us to say "please" and "thank you" in our native language, why not expand your etiquette to another language? Spanish, for example, has its own set of magic words and phrases that can help you connect with others in a more polite manner. So why not incorporate "por favor" and "gracias" into your vocabulary, just as you would in English? Not only will it show your respect and appreciation, but it may also open doors to new cultural experiences and friendships.

English	Spanish	Pronunciation
Thanks / Thank you	Gracias	[grah-syahs]
Thanks a lot / Thank you very much	Muchas gracias	[moo-chahs grah-syahs]
You're welcome	De nada	[deh nah-dah]
Please	Por favor	[pohr fah-bohr]
Excuse me / Pardon me (to get someone's attention or to apologize to someone or for something you did)	Perdón	[pehr-dohn]

English	Spanish	Pronunciation
Excuse me / Pardon me (to ask for permission to go through a group of people)	**Con permiso, permiso**	*[kohn pehr-mee-soh]*
It's nothing	**No es nada**	*[noh ehs nah-dah]*
Excuse me (to get someone's attention or to apologize to someone for something you did)	**Disculpe**	*[dees-kool-peh]*

Now let's dive into some hands-on practice!

1.3. Practice

A. Choose the most appropriate response from the list on the right to the following greetings or expressions:

1. Muchas gracias _____
2. Buenos días _____
3. Perdón _____
4. ¿Qué tal? _____
5. Adiós _____
6. Buenas tardes _____
7. ¿Cómo está? _____

a. Muy buenas tardes.
b. Bien, gracias, ¿y usted?
c. De nada
d. Buenos días, ¿cómo está?
e. No es nada
f. Hasta luego
g. Bien, ¿y tú?

B. What might these people say to each other if they met or passed each other at the time given? There might be more than one possible answer.

1. Laura and Mathew at 2.00 p.m.
2. Mary and her boss at 7.00 a.m.
3. You and your friend at 12.00 a.m.
4. Joe and Ann at 10.00 p.m.
5. You and your Math teacher at 11 a.m.

C. **Match the situation with what you say if it happens. There might be more than one possible answer.**

Choices:

Permiso	No es nada	Disculpe	Perdón	De nada

1. You accidentally bump into a person on the street.
2. You're trying to squeeze your way out of a packed subway.
3. A waiter apologizes for spilling water on your shirt.
4. You're trying to reach the aisle at the movie theater to use the restroom.
5. You're trying to draw the cashier's attention at the supermarket, who's sitting with his back to you.
6. An elderly woman thanks you for helping her cross the street.

D. **Choose the most appropriate response to the following statements or questions**

1. Muchas gracias   Hasta luego
2. ¿Qué tal?   No es nada
3. ¿Cómo está?   Bien, ¿y tú?
4. Adiós   Muy bien, gracias
5. Disculpe   De nada

E. **Complete the following dialogue with the right greeting or phrase.**

1. YOU: Hola, Martín, ¿_____[1]?
2. MARTÍN: Bien, gracias, ¿_____[2] ?
3. YOU: Muy_____[3] .
4. MARTÍN: Adiós._____[4] mañana.
5. YOU: _____[5] .

> **Common Mistake**: Remember it's "Buen**o**s días," but "Buen**a**s tardes" and "Buen**a**s noches."

CHAPTER 2:

NOUNS AND ARTICLES

THE DOG AND A CAT

2.1 The Gender of Nouns and the Singular Definite Article

We covered pronouns, but what's a noun? Nouns are objects, places, and things.

In Spanish, nouns are called **sustantivos**, but don't worry you don't need to remember this just yet. Unlike English, all nouns in Spanish are either masculine or feminine. This doesn't mean that objects are perceived as having literal gender differences, of course, but rather, they are just classified into different groups.

Some of these are straightforward, such as **el hombre** and **la mujer,** which mean *the man* and *the woman* respectively. As you'd expect, **el hombre** is a masculine noun and **la mujer** is a feminine noun. Although they're different words, **el** and **la** both mean 'the' – they simply apply to different genders. You would never ever say 'la hombre' or 'el mujer' as it would be grammatically incorrect.

It's easy with people, but less easy with objects and places. To speak fluent Spanish, you'll need to get used to the genders of different nouns. For example, you'll need to remember that a book is masculine while a photograph is feminine.

The definite article (the) should always agree with the gender of the noun. This is a hard one for English speakers, because we only have one definite article—the—and don't have to worry about the rest!

Singular Masculine Nouns

So, is there a way to tell masculine from feminine nouns? Well, most masculine nouns end in **-o**.

As we mentioned earlier, the masculine singular noun uses the definite article **el**. This shows we are referring to just one of the things, places, or objects we are referring to. Don't worry about plural nouns for now, we'll get to those later.

The following table contains singular masculine nouns:

English	Spanish	Pronunciation
the man	el hombre	[ehl ohm-bre]
the friend (male)	el amigo	[ehl ah-mee-goh]
the boy	el niño	[ehl nee-nyoh]
the son	el hijo	[ehl ee-hoh]
the brother	el hermano	[ehl ehr-mah-noh]
the grandfather	el abuelo	[ehl ah-bweh-loh]
the uncle	el tío	[ehl tee-oh]
the cat	el gato	[ehl gah-toh]
the dog	el perro	[ehl peh-rroh]
the book	el libro	[ehl lee-broh]
the telephone	el teléfono	[ehl teh-leh-foh-noh]
the youngster	el muchacho	[ehl moo-chah-choh]

Some masculine nouns end in -e:

English	Spanish	Pronunciation
the tomato	el tomate	[ehl toh-mah-teh]
the coffee	el café	[ehl kah-feh]
the student	el estudiante	[ehl ehs-too-dyan-teh]

But some masculine nouns do not end in **-o**; they may end in a consonant like **l**, **r**, or **z**.

English	Spanish	Pronunciation
the animal	el animal	[ehl ah-nee-mahl]
the hospital	el hospital	[ehl ohs-pee-tahl]
the doctor	el doctor	[ehl dohk-tohr]
the hotel	el hotel	[ehl oh-tehl]
the train	el tren	[ehl trehn]
the pencil	el lápiz	[ehl lah-peeth]

Speak Abroad
Academy

Alright, so not *all* masculine nouns end in -o. Most of them do, but there are some exceptions. Here are some masculine nouns that end in **-a** or **-ma**. Regardless of how the word ends, you'll still need to use **el** if it's masculine.

English	Spanish	Pronunciation
the climate	el clima	*[ehl klee-mah]*
the program	el programa	*[ehl proh-grah-mah]*
the system	el sistema*	*[ehl sees-teh-mah]*
the map	el mapa	*[ehl mah-pah]*
the language	el idioma	*[ehl ee-dyoh-mah]*
the planet	el planeta	*[ehl plah-neh-tah]*
the problem	el problema	*[ehl proh-bleh-mah]*
the tourist	el turista	*[ehl too-rees-tah]*
the sofa	el sofá	*[ehl soh-fah]*

> **Tip: Be careful!** Many English speakers say "la sistema," thinking this word is feminine. Remember, it's "**el sistema**."

> **Tip**: Since there is no clear rule about what ending a noun should have to be masculine, you'll need to memorize which noun is what gender. Don't worry, this gets easier with practice!

Singular Feminine Nouns

On the other hand, feminine nouns usually end in **-a**. The feminine singular noun uses the definite article **la**. Please take a look at the following table containing singular feminine nouns:

English	Spanish	Pronunciation
the person	la persona	*[lah pehr-soh-nah]*
the woman	la mujer	*[lah moo-hehr]*
the mother	la madre	*[lah mah-dreh]*
the friend (female)	la amiga	*[lah ah-mee-gah]*
the girl	la niña	*[lah nee-nyah]*
the girl	la muchacha	*[lah moo-chah-chah]*
the daughter	la hija	*[lah ee-hah]*
the sister	la hermana	*[lah ehr-mah-nah]*

English	Spanish	Pronunciation
the grandmother	**la abuela**	*[lah ah-bweh-lah]*
the aunt	**la tía**	*[lah tee-ah]*
the cat (female)	**la gata**	*[lah gah-tah]*
the dog (female)	**la perra**	*[lah peh-rrah]*
the house	**la casa**	*[lah kah-sah]*
the food	**la comida**	*[lah koh-mee-dah]*
the chair	**la silla**	*[lah see-yah]*

Some feminine nouns end in **-ción, -sión, -dad, -tad, or -tud**.

the conversation	**la conversación**	*[lah kohn-behr-sah-syohn]*
the television	**la televisión**	*[lah teh-leh-bee-syohn]*
the truth	**la verdad**	*[lah behr-dahd]*
the city	**la ciudad**	*[lah syoo-dahd]*
The drugstore	**la farmacia**	*[lah fahr-mah-thyah]*
the friendship	**la amistad**	*[lah ah-mees-tahd]*

While other feminine nouns end in **-o**!

the photograph	**la foto**	*[lah foh-toh]*
the hand	**la mano**	*[lah mah-noh]*
the radio	**la radio**	*[lah rrah-dyoh]*
the motorcycle	**la moto**	*[lah moh-toh]*

Again, since many feminine nouns don't follow a regular pattern, you need to learn each noun with its article, so you don't make mistakes like saying, "el mano," when it should be "**la mano**."

2.1. Practice

What's the appropriate masculine or feminine form of the definite article (the) for each noun? And while you're at it, try translating the word to see if you remember the meaning!

1. _____ foto
2. _____ hospital
3. _____ televisión
4. _____ casa
5. _____ libro

6. _____ ciudad
7. _____ conversación
8. _____ hijo
9. _____ planeta
10. _____ amigo

11.	_____ mapa		16.	_____ persona
12.	_____ programa		17.	_____ animal
13.	_____ sistema		18.	_____ comida
14.	_____ problema		19.	_____ mano
15.	_____ hotel		20.	_____ teléfono

> **Common Mistake:** The noun día (day) ends in -a but is masculine: el día (the day). So don't say, la día!

2.2 Plural Nouns and the Plural Definite Article

Plural Nouns

So far, we've only covered singular nouns. That is, just one object, place, or thing. But what if you wanted to refer to multiple friends, not just one friend? Or many books, not just a single book? This is where plural nouns come in.

In English, we usually indicate that there is *more* than one thing by adding "s" to the end of the word, like 'friends' or 'books.' In Spanish, plurality is also indicated by modifying the *ending* of the word.

If the Spanish singular noun ends in a vowel, like **amigo** (friend) or **mesa** (table), then we indicate plurality by ending the word with **-s.** So, in this case...

Amigo → Amigos

Mesa → Mesas

If you're referring to more than one friend, you would then use the word **amigos,** and for more than one table, you would use **mesas.**

If the Spanish singular noun ends up with a consonant (except for 'z') instead of a vowel, like **animal** (animal) or **ciudad** (city), then in this instance, we indicate plurality by ending the word with **-es.** So this would look like...

Animal → Animales

Ciudad → Ciudades

When you're talking about multiple animals, you would use the word **animales,** and for multiple cities, you would use the word **ciudades.**

Now, let's look at the final way of pluralizing a noun. If the Spanish singular noun ends in a 'z,' such as **lápiz** (pencil) or **nariz** (nose), we indicate plurality by **removing the 'z'** and ending the word with **-ces.** For example...

Lápiz → Lápices

Nariz → Narices

Hopefully, you're getting the hang of this by now! If you're referring to multiple pencils, you'd use the word **lápices.** And for multiple noses, you would use the word **narices**.

You might notice that something is missing – the definite article. How do we say 'the tables' or 'the cities?

Just like the nouns, the definite articles are also modified to indicate plurality. We must also keep in mind the gender of the noun!

The masculine definite article **el** becomes **los.**

The feminine definite article **la** becomes **las.**

For example...

El amigo → los amigos

La casa → las casas

> **Tip:** Remember that in Spanish, if we're referring to multiple people that consist of both females and males, we use the masculine plurality by default. So, you would use the term **los amigos** when referring to your friends if your friends include both males and females.
>
> To clarify...
>
> **Los amigos =** male friends OR male friends + female friends

> **Tip**: Keep in mind that, just like in English, we don't always need to use the definite article. In English, the definite article is the word 'the,' and in Spanish, this is **el, la, los,** and **las.** So, when do you need to use the definite article?
>
> First, let's just quickly go over what the point of the definite article is. Let's use an English example.
>
> If you have a salad in your fridge that you really need to eat before it goes bad, you would say 'I need to eat *the* salad.' Using the definite article indicates that you have a specific salad in mind. It's already there and it's just waiting to be eaten!
>
> However, if you feel like you've been eating too much fast food lately, you might say 'I need to eat *a* salad.' In this case, you don't have a specific salad in mind, you just need to eat any salad. That's why we call it the *definite* article because there is more certainty and specificity implied.

> These rules about when to use the definite article also apply to Spanish – but a couple of extra ones are added on top. Let's summarize!
>
> In Spanish, the definite article (**el, la, los, las**) is used...
>
> To refer to a specific person or thing. **La mujer de Adán es Eva** (*Eve is Adam's woman*).
>
> To refer to something in a broad sense. It's the article that precedes the noun. **Me gusta la carne** (*I like meat*) or **me gusta la musica** (*I like music*)
>
> To refer to parts of your own body. The possessive is already established in the verb, so it's not necessary to repeat it. You only need an article. **Me rompí el brazo** (*I broke my arm*)

Time to practice what we've learned—let's dive in!

2.2. Practice

A. Write the plural version of each singular noun. When you finish, read each pair out loud.

1. El hombre _____
2. La amiga _____
3. La conversación _____
4. El animal _____
5. El sistema _____

6. El niño _____
7. La casa _____
8. El tren _____
9. La ciudad _____
10. El doctor _____

B. Write the singular version of each plural noun. When you finish, read each pair out loud.

1. Las verdades _____
2. Las televisiones _____
3. Las manos _____
4. Las perras _____

5. Los lápices _____
6. Las niñas _____
7. Las radios _____
8. Las comidas _____

2.3 The Indefinite Article

So, we've already talked about the definite article. What about the indefinite article? Remember when we talked about the difference between 'I need to eat *the* salad' and 'I need to eat *a* salad'? As you can probably guess, it's in 'a salad' where the indefinite article is used. We use the indefinite article to refer to a thing that is non-specific.

In English, the indefinite article is *a* or *an*. In Spanish, the indefinite articles are...

Masculine, singular: **un** (*a/an*)

Masculine, plural: **unos** (*some*)

Feminine, singula: **una** (*a/an*)

Feminine, plural: **unas** (*some*)

For example:

Una amiga [uhnah ah-mee-gah] *(a female friend)* → **unas amigas** [uhnahs ah-mee-gahs] *(some female friends)*

Un hijo [uhn ee-hoh] *(a son)* → **unos hijos** [uhnohs ee-hohs] *(some sons)*

To summarize, you only use the indefinite article (**un, unos, una, unas**) when:

↪ You want to identify someone or something as part of a class or group: **es un animal** (*it's an animal*).

↪ You want to refer to something in a non-specific way: **un bote es para navegar** (*a boat is for sailing*) or **es una mujer joven** (*She's a young woman*).

Quick Recap

	MASCULINE SINGULAR NOUNS	MASCULINE PLURAL NOUNS	FEMININE SINGULAR NOUNS	FEMININE PLURAL NOUNS
DEFINITE ARTICLES	**el** amigo (the male friend)	**los** amigos (the male friends)	**la** amiga (the female friend)	**las** amigas (the female friends)
INDEFINITE ARTICLES	**un** amigo (a male friend)	**unos** amigos (some male friends or some female and male friends)	**una** amiga (a female friend)	**unas** amigas (some female friends)

Tip: Un and **una** (*a* and *an*) can mean *one* as well as *a* or *an*. You will understand which one it means based on the context. For example, **Un** niño (*a boy*) vs. Compro **un** tomate (*I buy one tomato*).

Ready to flex those newfound skills? It's practice time!

2.3. Practice

A. Turn these singular nouns with indefinite articles into plural nouns with their indefinite articles.

1. un abuelo: _____
2. una conversación: _____
3. un perro: _____
4. una mujer: _____
5. un estudiante: _____

6. un doctor: _____
7. un hotel: _____
8. un tren: _____
9. un lápiz: _____
10. una ciudad: _____

B. Translate the following:

1. The (male and female) students: _____
2. The planets _____
3. A (female) doctor _____
4. Some photographs _____
5. The language _____
6. The tourists _____
7. Some (male and female) friends _____
8. A tomato _____
9. The conversation _____
10. Some truths _____

C. Complete the sentences with **el, la, los, las** or **un, una, unos, unas**

> **Tip: de + el = del.** When **de** (*of*) is followed by **el** (*the*), the words contract to **del** (*of the*), so if the question asks "**de**" followed by the answer "**el**", you can add an "**l**" in the answer space, to make it "**del**"

1. _____ casa de Juan.
2. Encontré (*I found*) _____ moneda (*coin*).
3. Es _____ cabeza (*head*) de _____ león.
4. Eso es _____ huella (*footprint*).
5. Son _____ amigas de mi hermana (*they are some friends of my sisters*)
6. Me gusta _____ pollo (I like chicken).
7. Llevo _____ pastel a tu casa (*I'm taking a cake to your house*).
8. Pedro compra _____ bebidas para la fiesta (*Pedro is buying the drinks for the party*).

D. **Do you remember what these nouns are in English? Remember to translate them with the definite or indefinite article that precedes them.**

1. El libro _____
2. La casa _____
3. Las flores _____
4. El muchacho _____
5. Los hermanos _____
6. El café_____
7. El tren _____
8. Los planetas _____

9. Un gato _____
10. Unos perros _____
11. El teléfono _____
12. Las manos _____
13. Un programa _____
14. Unos sistemas _____
15. Los libros _____
16. La ciudad _____

E. **Circle the right answer:**

1. [La / Una] madre de Tomás es simpática.
2. Quiero [los / unos] libros para leer.
3. Quiero [la / una] televisión nueva.
4. [Él / un] gato es un animal independiente.
5. Rompió (*he broke*) [la / una] ventana de la casa.
6. Me gustan [las / unas] flores.
7. Hablé (*I spoke*) con [el / un] director del colegio.
8. Teresa encontró [el / un] gato.
9. Metí (*I put*) [las / unas] llaves (*keys*) en la cartera (*purse*).

F. **Complete these sentences with the right definite or indefinite article (el/la/los/las/un/una/unos/unas)**

1. Washington es _____ ciudad en Estados Unidos.
2. Hudson es _____ calle (*street*) de tu casa.
3. Bogotá es _____ capital de Colombia.
4. _____ casa de Elena es grande.
5. _____ Papa (*Pope*) vive en Roma.
6. Necesito (*I need*) _____ chaqueta (*jacket*) roja.
7. ¿Tienes _____ llaves (*keys*) de la casa?
8. Vi (*I saw*) _____ león (*lion*) grande en el zoológico (*zoo*).

CHAPTER 3:

DESCRIBING PEOPLE AND THINGS
BROWN DOG AND BLACK CAT

3.1 Descriptive Adjectives

Remember what a noun is? It's a person, place, or thing, like 'house' or 'table.'

Sometimes it isn't enough to simply mention the object or subject – sometimes, it's necessary to describe the object or subject. This is where adjectives come in. We use adjectives to describe the nouns we're talking about. For example, we could say that a person is fat or thin – or that a table is big or small.

In Spanish, we usually put the adjective *after* the noun that we're describing.

So, to say 'big table,' this would look like **mesa <u>grande</u>**. As you can guess, the word **grande** means big and it is an adjective.

Adjectives are also used to describe other qualities, like the nationality of something or someone. For example, to say 'Spanish food,' we would say **comida <u>Española</u>** *[komeedah ehs-pah-nyohlah]*.

Although we usually put the adjective after the noun, there is one instance when we put the descriptor *before* the noun. And this is when we're describing the quantity of something. For example, when we say, 'few pencils,' this would be **<u>pocos</u> lápices.**

Adjectives won't always have the same ending. They will depend on

⊃   Gender of the noun

⊃   The singularity or plurality of the noun

So, if you have a feminine singular noun like **la foto** (the photo), you will need to use a feminine singular adjective like **hermosa** (beautiful) to describe it. In this case, you would say **la foto hermosa** to say, 'the beautiful photo.'

Singular form of adjectives

Adjectives that end in **-o** are masculine and agree with a masculine noun. For example: El amigo **bueno** (*the good friend*). Keep in mind that Spanish adjectives are the last words in the sentence, since they usually go after the noun.

English	Spanish	Pronunciation
The tall student	El estudiante alto	[ehl ehs-too-dyahn-teh ahl-toh]
The short boy	El niño bajo	[ehl nee-nyoh bah-hoh]
The good brother	El hermano bueno	[ehl ehr-mah-noh bweh-noh]
The bad dog	El perro malo	[ehl peh-rroh mah-loh]
The fat cat	El gato gordo	[ehl gah-toh gohr-doh]
The thin uncle	El tío flaco	[ehl tee-oh flah-koh]
The friendly boy	El niño simpático	[ehl nee-nyoh seem-pah-tee-koh]
The unfriendly youngster	El muchacho antipático	[ehl moo-chah-choh ahn-tee-pah-tee-koh]
The small book	El libro pequeño	[ehl lee-broh peh-keh-nyoh]
The hard working grandfather	El abuelo trabajador	[ehl ah-bweh-loh trah-bah-hah-dohr]
The beautiful sofa	El sofá hermoso	[ehl sow-fuh ehr-moh-soh]
The old man	El hombre viejo	[ehl ohm-breh byeh-hoh]
The mischievous boy	El niño travieso	[ehl nee-nyoh trah-byeh-soh]

But what if you're not referring to a masculine noun? Sometimes, you need to describe a female student as tall, not just a male student!

In this case, adjectives change the **-o** to **-a** when they describe a feminine noun. For example: La niña **buena** (*the good girl*).

English	Spanish	Pronunciation
The tall (female) student	La estudiante alta	[lah ehs-too-dyahn-teh ahl-tah]
The short girl	La niña baja	[lah nee-nyah bah-hah]
The good sister	La hermana buena	[lah ehr-mah-nah bweh-nah]
The bad (female) dog	La perra mala	[lah peh-rrah mah-lah]
The fat (female) cat	La gata gorda	[lah gah-tah gohr-dah]
The thin aunt	La tía flaca	[lah tee-ah flah-kah]
The friendly girl	La niña simpática	[lah nee-nyah seem-pah-tee-kah]
The unfriendly (female) youngster	La muchacha antipática	[la moo-chah-chah ahn-tee-pah-tee-kah]
The small house	La casa pequeña	[lah kah-sah peh-keh-nyah]

Describing people and things

Speak Abroad
Academy

English	Spanish	Pronunciation
The hardworking grandmother	**La abuela trabajadora**	[lah ah-bweh-lah trah-bah-hah-dohra]
The beautiful city	**La ciudad hermosa**	[lah thyoo-dahd ehr-moh-sah]
The old woman	**La mujer vieja**	[lah moo-hehr byeh-hah]

Sometimes, you don't need to change the ending of an adjective. This makes it a little easier!

If the adjective ends in **-e** (inteligente) or in a consonant like **-l** (fiel), they will have the same form whether they describe a feminine or masculine noun: hombre **fiel** (loyal man) and mujer **fiel** (loyal woman).

English	Spanish	Pronunciation
The excellent book	**El libro excelente**	[ehl lee-broh ehks-theh-lehn-teh]
The poor man	**El hombre pobre**	[ehl ohm-breh poh-breh]
The big planet	**El planeta grande**	[ehl plah-neh-tah grahn-deh]
The loyal friend	**El amigo fiel**	[ehl ah-mee-goh fyehl]
The weak boy	**El niño débil**	[ehl nee-nyoh deh-beel]
The difficult conversation	**La conversación difícil**	[lah kohn-behr-sah-thyohn dee-fee-theel]
The easy issue	**El tema fácil**	[ehl teh-mah fah-theel]
The strong woman	**La mujer fuerte**	[lah moo-hehr fwehr-teh]
The excellent food	**La comida excelente**	[lah koh-mee-dah ehks-theh-lehn-teh]
The kind lady	**La señora amable**	[lah seh-nyoh-rah ah-mah-bleh]
The (male) young student	**El estudiante joven**	[ehl ehs-too-dyahn-teh hoh-behn]
The intelligent (female) doctor	**La doctora inteligente**	[lah dohk-tohr een-teh-lee-hehn-teh]
The cheerful girl	**La niña alegre**	[lah nee-nyah ah-leh-greh]

Now, let's introduce another rule.

Remember when I said that the Spanish adjective *usually* goes after the noun? If you want to emphasize the quality of something or add an emotional charge to a description, you can sometimes place the adjective before the noun. In this case, the adjective will be shortened.

For example, **bueno, malo**, and **grande** may all appear before the noun. When **bueno** and **malo** precede a masculine singular noun, **bueno** will become **buen** and **malo** will become **mal.**

Un libro bueno and **un buen libro** both mean *'a good book,'* but you may choose to say **un buen libro** to emphasize just how much you enjoyed this excellent book.

On the other hand, if you thought a program was particularly bad, you might choose to say **un mal programa** instead of **un programa malo.** They both mean 'a bad program,' but the former places more of an emotional charge on the word 'bad.'

Sometimes, this can slightly change the meaning of the adjectives in question.

When **grande** is placed after a noun, it simply means large or big, like in the sentence **una casa grande** (*a large house*). When it is placed before a singular noun instead of after, it is shortened to **gran** and means impressive or great. You could even say **un gran doctor** to say, 'a great doctor.'

Time to get your learning hat on; it's time for some hands-on practice!

3.1. Practice

A. Translate the English adjective into its Spanish equivalent. Make sure it matches the noun.

1. La niña _____ (*tall*)
2. El hombre _____ (*poor*)
3. El perro _____ (*loyal*)
4. La muchacha _____(*beautiful*)
5. El problema _____(*difficult*)
6. El niño _____ (*good*)
7. El abuelo _____ (*happy*)
8. El libro _____ (*interesting*)
9. La amistad_____ (*strong*)
10. La mano _____ (*weak*)

B. Translate the English adjective into its Spanish equivalent. Make sure it matches the noun.

1. La tía _____ (*short*)
2. La comida _____ (*excellent*)
3. La ciudad _____ (*small*)
4. El tío _____ (*friendly*)
5. El hotel _____ (*old*)
6. El gato _____ (*bad*)
7. La amiga _____ (*intelligent*)
8. La perra _____ (*loyal*)
9. El muchacho _____ (*hardworking*)
10. El turista _____ (*fat*)

C. Write the opposite adjectives to the one in the sentences below.

1. El tema fácil _____
2. El niño bajo _____
3. El restaurante malo _____
4. La niña antipática _____
5. El perro pequeño _____
6. El hombre fuerte _____

Plural Form of Adjectives

I'm sure you guessed that this was coming! When the noun is plural and refers to multiple things, the adjectives must be modified to agree with the plurality.

A singular adjective that ends in a vowel adds **-s** to form the plural:

Alto → altos (*tall*)

Pobre → pobres (*poor*)

A singular adjective that ends In a consonant, adds **–es** to indicate plurality

Fácil → fáciles (*easy*)

Joven → jovenes (*young*)

Ready to apply what you've learned? Let's practice!

3.1. Practice

D. Write the plural form of each of the following nouns and adjectives.

1. El tomate grande _____
2. El hombre alto _____
3. El perro inteligente _____
4. La niña fuerte _____
5. La persona trabajadora _____
6. La ciudad pequeña _____
7. El gato flaco _____
8. La mujer alegre _____
9. El libro difícil _____
10. La comida excelente _____

E. Complete the sentence with the correct form of the adjectives:

1. Los libros _____ (excelente)
2. La abuela _____ (trabajador)
3. La ciudad _____ (hermoso)
4. Los libros _____ (pequeño)

5. Los sofás _____ (hermoso)
6. Las hermanas _____ (bueno)
7. Los gatos _____ (gordo)
8. Los niños _____ (simpático)

3.2 Adjectives of Nationality

As we mentioned earlier, nationalities are also adjectives. They describe the quality of a thing or person. In Spanish, the word for a country's language is sometimes the same as the word for the singular form of their nationality.

For example: **el inglés (English), el español (Spanish), and el francés (French).**

This is similar to English, where the language 'English' uses the same word as the nationality 'English.' The same goes for 'Spanish' and 'French.'

In the Spanish examples above, you'll notice that all three languages/nationalities are masculine. This means that the words for language and nationality are only interchangeable when the noun is masculine. When the noun is feminine, however, the adjective (in this case, the nationality) must be modified to a feminine form.

This means that you would say **ella es <u>francesa</u>** (she is French) when you're talking about a female French person.

But if you were talking about a male French person, you could say **él es <u>francés</u>**, using the same word for the language itself.

English	Spanish	Pronunciation
Spanish	**español**	*[ehs-pah-nyohl]*
English	**inglés**	*[eeng-glehs]*
French	**francés**	*[frahn-thehs]*
German	**alemán**	*[ah-leh-mahn]*
Italian	**italiano**	*[ee-tah-lyah-noh]*
Portuguese	**portugués**	*[pohr-too-gehs]*
North American/American	**norteamericano**	*[nohr-teh-ah-meh-ree-kah-noh]*

Tip: In Spanish, you do not capitalize the names of languages and adjectives of nationality, though you do capitalize the names of countries and cities.

Let's make it real! Time for some practical exercises to solidify your skills.

3.2. Practice

Write the nationality next to each noun, making it match in gender and number.

1. La Estatua de la Libertad es _____.
2. La Torre Eiffel es _____.
3. El Big Ben es _____.
4. La Torre de Pisa es _____.
5. El Museo El Prado es _____.
6. Angela Merkel es _____.

3.3 Describing a Person

In Spanish, there's more than one way to write a descriptive sentence – just like in English. You can say 'the intelligent woman' or you can say 'the woman is intelligent.'

So far, we've only discussed how to say, 'the intelligent woman,' i.e. **la mujer inteligente.** Now, let's try a different way of using these descriptors.

To say someone or something *is* something, you use the Spanish word **es.** This means that 'the woman is intelligent' would become '**la mujer es inteligente**.'

Of course, you don't always have to specify 'the woman,' you can also use pronouns to indicate who you're talking about. In this case, just replace the noun with the pronoun. To simply say 'she is intelligent,' you translate this to '**ella es inteligente.**'

Fortunately, the words 'is' and **es** are only different by one letter, so this should be somewhat easy to remember! You'll also be glad to hear that you use the word **es** no matter if you're talking about a feminine or masculine noun. For example, 'he is friendly' would be '**El es simpático**.'

Got the concept down? Now, let's apply it with some good old practice!

3.3. Practice

A. Which adjectives are the most appropriate for each sentence?

1. La tía María es _____ (bajos / inteligente / hermosa/ fuertes)
2. El señor García es _____ (trabajadora / alegre / interesante / pobres)
3. La ciudad es _____ (grande / interesante / viejo / hermoso)
4. El niño es _____ (malos / bueno / flaca / simpático)
5. Los gatos son _____ (bueno / malos / blancos / negro)
6. Los perros son _____ (simpáticos / alegres / fuerte / inteligente)

B. **Using the word es, choose two adjectives to describe the following people/things:**

Adjectives			
grande	limpia	simpático	gordo
interesante	trabajadora	bueno	hermoso

1. Mi padre es _____
2. Mi madre es _____
3. Mi hermano es _____
4. Mi gato es _____
5. Mi perro es _____
6. Mi ciudad es _____

C. **Translate the following:**

1. Monique is French: Monique es _____
2. Carlo is Italian: Carlo es _____
3. Helmut is German: Helmut es _____
4. Sofía is Spanish: Sofía es _____
5. María is Portuguese: María es _____
6. Ted is English: Ted es_____

D. **Do you remember where these famous people are from?**

1. Pablo Picasso es _____
2. Emmanuel Macron es _____
3. Daniel Craig es _____
4. Marco Polo es _____
5. Antonio Banderas es _____
6. Miley Cyrus es _____

Common Error: Remember not to make the mistake of placing the adjectives before the subject when you speak Spanish.

Common Error: Remember not to make the mistake of placing the adjectives before the subject when you speak Spanish.

X   Don't say: Un **difícil** examen (*a difficult exam*)

✓   It should be: Un examen **difícil**

CHAPTER 4:

DESCRIBING THINGS
THE YELLOW BRICK ROAD

4.1 More Adjectives

Now let's break free from the rules for a moment! Join me on a journey of exploration; it's time to infuse some enchantment into your Spanish vocabulary and uncover the tapestry of the Spanish language, where every adjective is a brushstroke crafting vibrant portraits of the world, its people, and the experiences that surround you. Did you know Spanish is a language steeped in artistic heritage, producing masterpieces like Picasso's Guernica and Velázquez's Las Meninas? Therefore, it's important to immerse yourself in this linguistic canvas, letting the hues of Spanish enhance your expression. I mean how else can we describe the world around and within us in greater detail?

Here are some useful everyday adjectives that you'll need to know!

Descriptive Adjectives

English	Spanish	Pronunciation
fast	**rápido**	*[rrah-peeh-doh]*
slow	**lento**	*[lehn-toh]*
cheap	**barato**	*[bah-rah-toh]*
expensive	**caro**	*[kah-roh]*
famous	**famoso**	*[fah-moh-soh]*
long	**largo**	*[lahr-goh]*
short	**corto**	*[kohr-toh]*
young	**joven**	*[hoh-behn]*
elderly	**anciano**	*[ahn-thyah-noh]*
pretty	**lindo**	*[leen-doh]*
ugly	**feo**	*[feh-oh]*
happy	**feliz**	*[feh-leeth]*
sad	**triste**	*[trees-teh]*
rich	**rico**	*[rreeh-koh]*
new	**nuevo**	*[nweh-boh]*

English	Spanish	Pronunciation
blond	**rubio**	*[rroo-byoh]*
dark-haired / dark-skinned	**moreno**	*[moh-reh-noh]*
delicious	**sabroso**	*[sah-brroh-soh]*

I'm sure you're now wondering what these adjectives look like in a sentence? Let's use them with some nouns we used in prior chapters.

El problema fácil (*the easy problem*)

La moto rápida (*the fast motorcycle*)

La silla barata (*the cheap chair*)

La niña famosa (*the famous girl*)

La mujer feliz (*the happy woman*)

El hombre triste (*the sad man*)

El niño moreno (*the dark-skinned boy*)

La comida sabrosa (*the delicious food*)

La lección corta (*the short lesson*)

El tren largo (*the long train*)

Colors

Of course, colors are adjectives too – and they're extremely important ones. All the rules you've learned about adjectives so far also apply to colors. Treat them just like you would all the other adjectives you've learned and place them after the noun.

English	Spanish	Pronunciation
white	**blanco**	*[blahn-koh]*
black	**negro**	*[neh-groh]*
red	**rojo**	*[rroh-hoh]*
blue	**azul**	*[ah-thool]*
yellow	**amarillo**	*[ah-mah-ree-yoh]*
green	**verde**	*[behr-deh]*
grey	**gris**	*[grees]*
pink	**rosa/rosado**	*[rroh-sah] [rroh-sah-doh]*
brown	**marrón**	*[mah-rrohn]*
orange	**anaranjado/naranja**	*[ah-nah-rahn-hah-doh]* *[nah-rahn-hah]*

And here are some examples on how to use colors with a noun:

El planeta rojo *(the red planet)*

El lápiz negro *(the black pencil)*

El gato blanco *(the white cat)*

El sofá amarillo *(the yellow sofa)*

La silla verde *(the green chair)*

La moto azul *(the blue motorcycle)*

La casa rosada *(the pink house)*

La perra marrón *(the brown dog)*

To modify these colors for plurality or multiple nouns, add **-s** (if it ends in a vowel) or **-es** (if it ends in a consonant) to the end of each adjective. For example:

Los planetas rojos *(the red planets)*

Los lápices negros *(the black pencils)*

Los gatos blancos *(the white cats)*

Los sofás amarillos *(the yellow sofa)*

Las sillas verdes *(the green chairs)*

Las motos azules *(the blue motorcycles)*

Las casas rosadas *(the pink houses)*

Las perras marrones *(the brown dogs)*

No time to waste; let's jump straight into some practical exercises!

4.1. Practice

A. Let's practice nouns

It's a good idea to practice what you already know so far: nouns (Second Lesson) and adjectives (Third Lesson and Fourth Lesson). Find the right adjective for the following nouns according to the noun being masculine or feminine.

trabajadora - cara - interesante - moreno - difícil - rápido - feliz - inteligente - vieja - nuevo - fiel - alto - rico - nueva - fácil - barata - anciana - sabroso - marrón

1. La perra es _____.
2. El sofá es _____.
3. La muchacha es _____.
4. El tren es _____.
5. El niño es _____.
6. La televisión es _____.
7. El café es _____.
8. La persona es _____.
9. La casa es _____.
10. La abuela es _____.
11. El problema es _____.
12. La niña es _____.
13. El programa es _____.
14. El hombre es _____.
15. La moto es _____.
16. La silla es _____.
17. El idioma es _____.
18. El tomate es _____.

B.   Let's practice colors!

Complete the following phrases translating the color adjectives from English to Spanish.

1.   La flor _____ *(yellow)*
2.   La casa _____ *(blue)*
3.   La silla _____ *(orange)*
4.   La mano _____ *(white)*
5.   La gata _____ *(black)*
6.   El lápiz _____ *(gris)*
7.   El sofá _____ *(green)*
8.   El teléfono _____ *(pink)*
9.   El perro _____ *(brown)*
10. El tomate _____ *(red)*

C.   Answer these questions according to the example, by matching the adjectives to the noun.

Example: El perro es inteligente. ¿Y los gatos? <u>También son inteligentes.</u>

1.   La madre es amable. ¿Y el padre? _____
2.   El examen de matemáticas *(math)* es fácil. ¿Y el examen de literatura *(literature)*? _ _____
3.   Las tías son trabajadoras. ¿Y los tíos? _____
4.   El perro es gordo. ¿Y los gatos? _____
5.   Los abuelos son buenos. ¿Y la abuela? _____
6.   La hermana es fuerte. ¿Y los hermanos? _____

D.   Answer the following questions:

1.   Elena and Sofía are quite opposite. What is Sofía like?
     Elena es baja, perezosa, morena, infeliz y pobre, pero Sofía es
     _____

2.   Tomás and Martín's house are the opposite. What is Martín's house like?
     La casa de Tomás es pequeña, hermosa, nueva, barata y alta, pero la casa de Martín es _____

3.   Germán and Pablo are quite opposite. What is Pablo like?
     Germán es rico, inteligente, rubio, alto, trabajador y viejo, pero Pablo es
     _____

4.2 Demonstrative Adjectives

We've talked primarily about common adjectives so far. Now, let's talk about demonstrative adjectives. You've probably noticed that we're tossing around some very official linguistic terminology here. Let me just say that although it's important for you to be introduced to official terms like 'demonstrative adjectives,' you don't have to remember them *if you remember the rule itself*.

So, let's talk about demonstrative adjectives.

These are words like 'this' or 'that,' which draw attention to specific nouns (singular or plural). You know what purpose they serve in English, and it's essentially the same in Spanish.

When we use these words, they go *before* the noun, just like in English, and they also change if we're talking about multiple nouns. This is like the difference between 'this' and 'these.' For example, you would say **este perro** for 'this dog' and **estos perros** for 'these dogs.'

And of course, they also need to be modified if you're talking about a feminine noun, like for example, **esta casa** (this house) and **estas casas** (these houses). Consider the table below:

this	**este**	*[ehs-teh]*	**esta**	*[ehs-tah]*
these	**estos**	*[ehs-tohs]*	**estas**	*[ehs-tahs]*
that	**ese**	*[eh-seh]*	**esa**	*[eh-sah]*
	aquel	*[ah-kehl]*	**aquella**	*[ah-keh-yah]*
those	**esos**	*[eh-sohs]*	**esas**	*[eh-sahs]*
	aquellos	*[ah-keh-yohs]*	**aquellas**	*[ah-keh-yahs]*

> **Tip:** So, what's the distinction between "ese/esa" (that) and "aquel/aquella" (those)? It's akin to English! Use "esa/ese" when referring to things or people closer to you. On the other hand, go for "aquel/aquella" for things or people that are further away.

Time to transition from theory to action! Let's practice and perfect those skills.

4.2. Practice

A. Beatriz and her friend go shopping. Check out what they say about the clothes, using the demonstrative adjective **este** in the correct form. Use **es** (*is*) or **son** (*are*) depending on whether the subject is singular or plural.

Example: vestido (dress) / rojo (red) → **Este** vestido es rojo.

1. camisa (shirt) / linda → _____
2. zapatos (shoes) / caros → _____
3. suéter (sweater) / lana (wool) → _____

4. vestidos (dresses) / seda (silk) → _____
5. pantalones (pants) / baratos →_____

B. Now use the demonstrative adjective ese in the correct form.

Example: medias (socks) / largas → **Esas** medias son largas.

1. blusa (*blouse*) / blanca → _____
2. camiseta (*t-shirt*) / roja → _____
3. faldas (*skirt*) / cortas → _____
4. chaqueta (*jacket*) / **muy*** barata _____
5. zapatillas deportivas (*sneakers*) / hermosas_____

*Muy: Is an adverb that means **very**. Adverbs go before adjectives and verbs. Check out some more adverbs here:

muy (*very*)	+ adjective/adverb	Esas flores son **muy** hermosas. (*Those flowers are very beautiful.*)
mucho (*a lot*)	+ verb	Carlos viaja **mucho**. (*Carlos travels a lot.*)
bastante (*quite*)	+ adjective/adverb/verb	Ella camina **bastante** rápido. (*She walks quite fast.*)
poco (*not a lot*)	+ adjective/adverb/verb	Martín come **poco**. (*Martín doesn't eat a lot.*)
demasiado (*too much*)	+ adjective/adverb/verb	Elena habla **demasiado**. (*Elena talks too much.*)

C. Complete these sentences with este, ese, or aquel.

1. ¿Quién (*Who*) es _____ (that) doctor? (This) _____ doctor es un cardiólogo (*cardiologist*).
2. _____ (This) planeta es muy grande.
3. _____ (that over there) casa es hermosa.
4. _____ (that over there) tren es grande.
5. _____ (that) moto es nueva.
6. _____ (that) joven es simpático.
7. El estudiante es _____ (that over there) muchacho.

D. Complete each sentence with the correct form of **este, esta, estos, estas**. Next answer in the reverse, using the adjective that means the opposite. Example: **¿Es bueno** _____ **profesor?** _____ **: ¿Es bueno este profesor? No, es malo.**

1. ¿Es feliz _____ niña? _____ .

2. ¿Son ricos _____ muchachos? _____ .

3. ¿Es feo _____ perro? _____ .

4. ¿Son viejos _____ edificios? _____ .

5. ¿Es anciana _____ mujer? _____ .

6. ¿Son fuertes _____ muchachas? _____ .

7. ¿Es grande _____ casa? _____ .

8. ¿Es alto _____ niño? _____ .

4.3 Describing People and Adjectives in the Plural Form

Remember when we talked about using **es** to describe a singular noun? Like, for example, **la mujer es inteligente** to say, 'the woman is intelligent'?

It also becomes necessary to describe plural nouns in the same way. In English, 'is' becomes 'are' when we're talking about plural nouns, like in the sentence 'the books are boring.'

In Spanish, **es** becomes **son.**

Instead of...

> **él es**: he (masculine) is

> **ella es**: she (feminine) is

You would say...

> **ellos son:** they (masculine) are

> **ellas son:** they (feminine) are

Just like **es**, you use the word **son** regardless of whether the noun is feminine or masculine.

For example:

They (a group of men) are thin → Ellos **son** flacos.

They (a group of women) are intelligent → Ellas **son** inteligentes.

Now, you know how to say 'he/she is' and 'they are'! Try and practice this with different adjectives.

Speak Abroad
Academy

Vocabulary: The Neighborhood

Time to expand your vocabulary! Let's look at some nouns that you'll encounter in your typical neighborhood, town, and city.

English	Spanish	Pronunciation
tree	**árbol**	*[ahr-bohl]*
flower	**flor**	*[flohr]*
street	**calle**	*[kah-yeh]*
post office	**correo**	*[koh-rreh-oh]*
fish store	**pescadería**	*[pehs-kah-deh-ree-ah]*
supermarket	**supermercado**	*[soo-pehr-mehr-kah-doh]*
office	**oficina**	*[oh-fee-thee-nah]*
car	**coche**	*[koh-cheh]*
theater	**teatro**	*[teh-ah-troh]*
salesperson	**dependiente**	*[deh-pehn-dyehn-teh]*
fruit and vegetable store	**verdulería**	*[behr-doo-leh-ree-ah]*
park	**parque**	*[pahr-keh]*
garden/yard	**jardín**	*[hahr-deen]*
school	**colegio**	*[koh-leh-hyoh]*
college/university	**universidad**	*[oo-nee-behr-see-dahd]*
movie theater	**cine**	*[thee-neh]*
church	**iglesia**	*[ee-gleh-syah]*
airport	**aeropuerto**	*[ah-eh-roh-pwehr-toh]*
museum	**museo**	*[moo-seh-oh]*
bar	**bar**	*[bahr]*
restaurant	**restaurante**	*[reehs-tow-rahn-teh]*
avenue	**avenida**	*[ah-beh-nee-dah]*
building	**edificio**	*[eh-dee-fee-thyoh]*

Describing things

Eager to see your knowledge in action? Let's practice and make it happen!

4.3. Practice

A.   Imagine you're showing your friend around your block from your car. Point out some places of interest, completing the sentences with the right form of **aquel** (*that over there*): **aquel, aquella, aquellos, aquellas.**

   1.   _____ casa es muy grande.
   2.   _____ edificio (*building*) es el correo (*post office*) y _____ árbol es muy viejo.
   3.   _____ calle (*street*) es nueva y _____ perros son malos.
   4.   _____ avenida es ancha.

B.   Rewrite these sentences using the right form of the demonstrative adjective, of the verb *to be* (**es** or **son**, depending on whether the subject is singular or plural), according to the form of the adjective (singular or plural).

Example: Este / calles / es / larga: Est**as** calle**s son** larga**s**.

   1.   Este / sistema / es / excelente _____
   2.   Este / pescaderias / es/ caro _____
   3.   Este / ciudad / es / hermoso _____
   4.   Este / teatro / es/ pequeño _____
   5.   Ese / oficinas / es / nuevo _____
   6.   Ese / coches / es / amarillo _____

Common Error: When using the word **persona**, avoid using a masculine adjective, even if the sex of the person you are referring to is male. **Persona** always agrees with a **feminine adjective**:

José es una persona bueno. X

José es una **persona** buena.✓

Martín es una persona trabajador. X

Martín es una **persona** trabajadora. ✓

Luis es una persona simpático. X

Luis es una **persona** simpática. ✓

CHAPTER 5:

THE VERB SER (TO BE)
TO BE OR NOT TO BE

Present Tense of Ser

Remember the words **es** and **son**? They mean 'is' and 'are,' which are essentially the same thing, but one is singular and the other is plural. The Spanish words **es** and **son** are all rooted in the same Spanish verb **ser**, which means 'to be.'

In English, we use the word **es** for basically everything. You use it to say both 'the car is red' (description) and 'the car is here' (location), even though you're describing different types of attributes about the car.

In Spanish, you wouldn't use the same word for different types of descriptions.

Yes, you can say **el coche es rojo** (the car is red), but you can't use the same word to indicate the location of the car.

To indicate location, you would say **el coche está aquí** (the car is here).

Let's look at the two verbs in these sentences, **es** and **está**. While **es** is rooted in the verb **ser**, which means 'to be,' **está** is rooted in the verb **estar**. And guess what? It also means 'to be'! That's right, in English, **ser** and **estar** both mean the same thing, but in Spanish, they describe different types of indications.

Before we learn more about **estar**, let's make sure you're familiar with all the forms of **ser**. You already know **es** and **son** ('is' and 'are'), which can be used to say **el/ella es** (he/she is) and **ellos/ellas son** (they are). But what if you wanted to say, 'we are' or 'I am'? To refer to different pronouns, you'll need to make modifications.

Let's take a look at these modifications and let's roll up our sleeves to get some practice in!

Mini Challenge

Read the following dialogue and use the table below (modifications for 'ser') to identify exactly what they're saying.

En la ciudad

TOMÁS: Disculpe, ¿este **es** el correo?

LUIS: Perdón, no **soy** de aquí.

TOMÁS: Ah, ¿de dónde **es** usted?

LUIS: **Soy** de otra ciudad. No **soy** de Madrid.

TOMÁS: Ah, **es** turista, como yo.

LUIS: Sí, **soy** turista. **Soy** de Estados Unidos. ¿Y usted?

TOMÁS: **Soy** de Francia.

LUIS: Ah. **Somos** dos turistas. Aquella señora **es** española. Ella **es** de acá.

Glossary:

De aquí: *from here*

¿De dónde…?: *Where… from?*

Otra: *another*

Como: *like*

Acá: *here*

---

ser *to be*			
yo	**soy**	nosotros/as	**somos**
tú	**eres**	vosotros/as	**sois**
usted		ustedes	
él	**es**	ellos	**son**
ella		ellas	

We mentioned that verbs meaning 'to be' are used to describe things in different ways. So, when exactly is **ser** (**soy, eres, es, son,** etc) used? Generally, **ser** is used to describe:

➲ The nature of something or someone   ➲ The identity of something or someone

➲ Time   ➲ Events

This means you would use **ser** in these ten situations:

1. **To** *describe*

Yo **soy** rubia	=	*I am blond*
Tú **eres** alto	=	*You're tall*
Él **es** joven	=	*He is young*
Ella **es** inteligente	=	*She is intelligent*
Somos simpáticos	=	*We are nice*
Vosotros **sois** solteros	=	*You all are single*
Ustedes **son** románticos	=	*You all are romantic*
Ellos **son** morenos	=	*They are dark-haired*

> **Tip:** Note that in Spanish you do not need to add the pronoun to a sentence—unless you want to stress it—because it is already included in the verb: **somos** simpáticos (*we are nice*).

2. **To** *indicate a profession*

Marcos **es** abogado	=	*Marcos is a lawyer*
Yo **soy** estudiante	=	*I am a student*
Ella **es** arquitecta	=	*She is an architect*
Somos doctores	=	*We are doctors*
Sois profesores	=	*You are professors*
Ustedes **son** gerentes	=	*You are managers*
Ellos **son** ingenieros	=	*They are engineers*

> **Tip**: Unlike English, Spanish omits the indefinite article **un/una** before an unmodified profession. For example: **Ellas son doctoras**. But if you modify the profession, you need to add the indefinite article: **Ellas son unas doctoras excelentes**.

3. **To** *indicate where someone comes from*

Yo **soy** de Perú	=	*I am from Peru*
Tú **eres** de Colombia	=	*You are from Colombia*
Él **es** de Nueva York	=	*He is from New York*
Usted **es** de España	=	*You are from Spain*
Nosotros **somos** de Italia	=	*We are from Italy*
Vosotros **sois** de Francia	=	*You are all from France*
Ellos **son** de Irlanda	=	*They are from Ireland*

4. **To** *identify specific attributes about a person, such as relationship, nationality, race, or religion*

Yo **soy** católica	=	*I am Catholic*
Tú **eres** argentino	=	*You are Argentinian*
Él **es** asiático	=	*He is Asian*
Somos solteros	=	*We are single*
Vosotros **sois** estudiantes y amigos	=	*You are students and friends*
Marcos y Luisa **son** amigos	=	*Marcos and Luisa are friends*

5. **To say** *what material something is made of*

La mesa **es** de madera	=	*The table is of wood* *(The table is made of wood)*
La casa **es** de ladrillos	=	*The house is of bricks* *(The house is made of bricks)*
La silla **es** de plástico	=	*The chair is of plastic* *(The chair is made of plastic)*
Los zapatos **son** de cuero	=	*The shoes are of leather* *(The shoes are made of leather)*
Las ventanas **son** de vidrio	=	*The windows are of glass* *(The windows are made of glass)*

6. **To say** *who something belongs to*

El perro **es** de María	=	*The dog is of María* *(The dog belongs to Maria)*
Los amigos **son** de Pedro	=	*The friends are of Pedro* *(The friends belong to Pedro).*

El libro **es** del muchacho	=	The book is of the boy (The book belongs to the boy)
La foto **es** de ella	=	The photograph is of her (The photograph belongs to her)
La moto **es** de ellos	=	The motorcycle is of them (The motorcycle belongs to them).

7. **To say for** *whom or for what something is intended*

La televisión **es** para ella	=	The television is for her
El lápiz **es** para ellos	=	The pencil is for them
La gata **es** para mi hermano	=	The (female) cat is for my brother

8. **To describe** *where an event takes place*

| La fiesta **es** en la casa de María | = | The party is in Maria's house |
| La ceremonia **es** en la universidad | = | The ceremony is at the university |

9. **To** *indicate a generalization*

| **Es** importante estudiar | = | It's important to study |

10. **To express time, dates, and days of the week.**

Son las 3:00 p.m.	=	It's 3:00 p.m.
Es el 14 de agosto	=	It's August 14th
Es lunes	=	It's Monday

> **Tip:** Note that in Spanish, the days of the week and the months of the year are NOT capitalized like in English.

Vocabulary: Types of Materials

English	Spanish	Pronunciation
paper	**papel**	*[pah-pehl]*
wood	**madera**	*[mah-deh-rah]*
glass	**vidrio**	*[bee-dryoh]*
plastic	**plástico**	*[plahs-tee-koh]*
metal	**metal**	*[meh-tahl]*
fabric	**tela**	*[teh-lah]*

The moment of truth has arrived—let's practice what we've learned!

5. Practice

A. Answer these questions about the dialogue "La ciudad" at the beginning of the lesson:

1. ¿De dónde es Luis? _____
2. ¿De dónde es Tomás? _____
3. ¿En qué ciudad están? _____
4. ¿Qué son Luis y Tomás? _____
5. ¿De dónde es la señora?_____

B. Where are these famous people from? Use the 3rd person singular of **ser** *(to be)* to say where they are from and what nationality they are.

Inglaterra (*England*)   Alemania (*Germany*)

Francia (*France*)   España (*Spain*)

Italia (*Italy*)   Portugal (*Portugal*)

México (*Mexico*)   Los Estados Unidos (*the United States*)

Example: David Beckham: Es de Inglaterra. Es inglés.

1. Luciano Pavarotti _____
2. Frida Kahlo _____
3. Johnny Depp _____
4. Albert Einstein _____
5. Coco Chanel _____
6. Rafael Nadal _____
7. Cristiano Ronaldo _____
8. Paul McCartney _____

C. Complete the following sentences with the appropriate form of ser and include in parentheses *why* you're using this verb:

- ☞ Description
- ☞ Profession
- ☞ Origin
- ☞ Identification
- ☞ Material something is made of
- ☞ Possession
- ☞ For whom something is intended
- ☞ Generalizations
- ☞ Where an event takes place
- ☞ Time, date, or day of the week

Example: El muchacho es simpático. (description)

1. Mick Jagger _____ inglés (_____)
2. Las sillas _____ de plástico (_____)
3. Nosotros _____ de Colombia (_____)
4. Las mesas _____ de madera (_____)

5. La comida _____ para la niña (_____)

6. _____ lunes (_____)

7. Marcos y Luis _____ abogados (_____)

8. La fiesta _____ en el club (_____)

9. El perro _____ de María (_____)

10. El libro _____ amarillo (_____)

11. _____ el 14 de febrero (_____)

D. **What are these objects made of? Example: ¿De qué es la mesa? Es de madera.**

1. ¿De qué es la botella (*bottle*)? _____

2. ¿De qué es la silla? _____

3. ¿De qué es la casa? _____

4. ¿De qué son los zapatos? _____

5. ¿De qué son las ventanas? _____

6. ¿De qué es el piso (*floor*)? _____

7. ¿De qué es el coche? _____

8. ¿De qué es la hoja (*page*)? _____

E. **Complete with the right form of the verb ser: es or son, depending on the subject.**

1. El perro _____ de María.

2. Los amigos _____ de Marcos.

3. La casa _____ de Teresa.

4. Las fotos _____ de los abuelos.

5. Los coches _____ de los tíos.

6. El gato _____ de María.

F. **Now let's try to use all the forms of the verb "to be". Complete the sentences with the right form of the verb "to be" (ser) and the place suggested in each case. Example: Yo (Perú) Yo soy de Perú**

1. Ellos (Alemania) _____

2. Tú y Alejandra (Argentina) _____

3. Vosotros (Colombia) _____

4. Nosotros (México) _____

5. Yo (Francia) _____

6. Felipe (Brasil) _____

G. **Use the right form of the verb ser:**

1. Usted _____ musulmán.

2. Yo _____ casada.

3. Nosotros _____ solteros.

4. Martín _____ chino.

5. Elena y Sofía _____ brasileñas.

Speak Abroad
Academy

6. Tú _____ blanco.

7. Vosotros _____ cristianos.

8. María _____ mexicana.

9. Tú y Martín _____ amigos.

H. **Translate the following sentences. Remember that you use es or son to express time, dates, and days of the week.**

1. It's three o'clock in the afternoon (tres de la tarde): _____

2. It's first of May (primero de mayo): _____

3. It's November 3rd (noviembre): _____

4. It's Wednesday (miércoles): _____

5. It's ten o'clock in the morning (diez de la mañana): _____

6. It's Sunday (domingo): _____

I. **Answer these questions with the appropriate form of ser:**

1. ¿Es usted simpático? _____

2. ¿Sois estudiantes? _____

3. ¿Es pequeña la casa de Mariana? _____

4. ¿De dónde es Elena? (Inglaterra)_____

5. ¿Qué es importante? (estudiar) _____

6. ¿Qué hora es? (4:00 p.m.) _____

J. **Rewrite these sentences contracting de + el. Example: El coche es de el señor Pérez:** **El coche es del señor Pérez.**

1. Los perros son de el niño: _____

2. El libro es de el colegio: _____

3. Aquella casa es de el hombre rico: _____

4. La moto es de el joven: _____

5. La comida es de el restaurante: _____

6. El coche es de el muchacho: _____

CHAPTER 6:

ESTAR (TO BE) AND TENER (TO HAVE)

I HAVE YOUR LOVE

6.1 Present Tense of Estar (*To Be*)

As we said in the previous chapter, **estar** also means 'to be.' However, it's used in different types of contexts and situations.

In Spanish, **estar** is used to express:

- location: ella **está** en la casa (*she is in the house*)
- health: él **está** enfermo (*he is sick*)
- changing mood or condition: **estoy** feliz (*I am happy*)
- personal opinion: la comida **está** deliciosa (*the food is delicious*)

Notice that what most of these situations have in common is that they are changeable. He is sick, but he might not be sick soon. It's a temporary state, not a permanent one. 'Sick' is his condition, but it's not his nature.

> **Tip:** When using **estar** for location, use the preposition **en + the article (el, la/los, las)**: **Sara está en la casa.**

estar *to be*			
yo	**estoy**	nosotros/as	**estamos**
tú	**estás**	vosotros/as	**estáis**
usted	**está**	ustedes	**están**
él		ellos	
ella		ellas	

Vocabulary: More Adjectives

Now let's learn some more adjectives to practice **estar**:

English	Spanish	Pronunciation
handsome	**guapo**	*[guah-poh]*
thin	**delgado**	*[dehl-gah-doh]*
stressed	**estresado**	*[ehs-treh-sah-doh]*
tired	**cansado**	*[kahn-sah-doh]*
happy	**contento**	*[kohn-tehn-toh]*
delicious	**delicioso**	*[deh-lee-thyoh-soh]*
sick	**enfermo**	*[ehn-fehr-moh]*
angry	**enojado**	*[eh-noh-hah-doh]*
clean	**limpio**	*[leem-pyoh]*
dirty	**sucio**	*[soo-thyoh]*
furious	**furioso**	*[foo-ryoh-soh]*
nervous	**nervioso**	*[nehr-byoh-soh]*
busy	**ocupado**	*[oh-koo-pah-doh]*
bored	**aburrido**	*[ah-boo-rree-doh]*
worried	**preocupado**	*[preh-oh-koo-pah-doh]*
open	**abierto**	*[ah-bee-ehr-toh]*
closed	**cerrado**	*[theh-rrah-doh]*

Got the concepts down? Now, let's apply them with some good old practice!

6.1. Practice

A. Write the appropriate form of **estar**. Say why you chose that option: **location, health, changing mood / condition, or personal opinion.**

1. París y Lyon _____ en Francia. (_____)
2. La niña _____ enferma. (_____)
3. _____ triste. (_____)
4. Juan _____ delgado. (_____)
5. Nosotros _____ aquí. (_____)
6. La comida _____ deliciosa. (_____)
7. Vosotros _____ contentos. (_____)
8. Tú _____ cansada. (_____)

B. And now, see if you can tell which verb to use, **ser** or **estar**, according to the meaning of each sentence, and match the verb to the subject in person and number.

Example: María y Juan están tristes.

1. La mesa y las sillas _____ sucias.
2. Él _____ abogado.
3. Nosotros _____ cansados.
4. _____ importante estudiar.
5. Vosotros _____ en la universidad.
6. Martín y Luis _____ inteligentes.
7. El café _____ para la mujer.
8. La ciudad _____ hermosa.
9. Tú _____ una turista.
10. Yo _____ de Guatemala.
11. La lección _____ fácil.
12. El niño _____ en el colegio.
13. Ustedes _____ contentos.
14. Nosotros _____ italianos.
15. Sara _____ triste.

C. Make complete sentences using the appropriate form of **ser** or **estar** + the words between the parentheses.

Example: La abuela (enferma) La abuela está enferma

1. Tim (español) _____
2. El restaurante (cerrado) _____
3. Las hijas de Pedro (rubias e inteligentes) _____
4. El problema (muy fácil) _____
5. El libro (interesante)_____
6. Tú (furioso) _____
7. La banana (amarilla) _____
8. Nosotros (felices) _____
9. La foto (silla) _____

> **Common Mistake:** Of course, since English speakers only have one verb (*to be*) to express all these situations, it's completely normal to be confused about when to use each verb when speaking or writing in Spanish. You'll get the hang of it with more practice!
>
> **X** Don't say: **Yo soy contenta.**
>
> **✓** The right way to say it is: **Yo estoy contenta.** (changing mood).

D. Write **ser** or **estar** according to whether the adjective refers to an inherent feature or a changing condition. Example: Él _____ triste → Él <u>está</u> triste (changing condition).

1. Ella _____ inteligente.
2. Él _____ estudioso.
3. Paula _____ furiosa.
4. Las abogadas _____ ocupadas.
5. La mesa _____ sucia.
6. El anciano _____ cansado.
7. El anciano _____ simpático.
8. La niña _____ nerviosa.

Summary of the Uses of Ser	
To describe	**La flor es hermosa**
To indicate a profession	**Yo soy abogada**
To indicate someone's origin/nationality	**Ellos son de México**
To identify inherent qualities about a person	**Él es inteligente**
To say what material something is made of	**La silla es de plástico**
To say who something belongs to	**El libro es de la niña**
To say for whom something is intended	**El perro es para él**
To describe where an event takes place	**La fiesta es en la casa**
To use a generalization	**Es importante estudiar**
To express time, dates, and days of the week	**Es martes** (It's Tuesday)

Summary of the Uses of Estar	
To express location	**Yo estoy en el restaurante**
To describe health	**María está enferma**
To express a changing mood or condition	**Luis está muy ocupado**
To express a personal opinion	**La universidad está bien**

Common Mistake:

Keep in mind that **ser** is used to express **inherent** qualities of a person, such as...

Luisa es cariñosa. Luisa has a sweet-loving character. That's her nature. She is nice because that's who she is.

Estar is used to express a **transitory** condition, such as...

Luisa está cansada. Luisa is tired now, but she won't be after she rests. ✔

Don't say X	Say ✓
Luisa está cariñosa.	Luisa es cariñosa.
Luisa es cansada.	Luisa está cansada.
Yo soy cansado.	Yo estoy cansado.
Mi papá es en el supermercado.	Mi papá está en el supermercado.
Él está un doctor.	Él es un doctor.

Then again, many adjectives can be used with either **ser** or **estar**, depending on the exact message that you're trying to convey. But as a rule, **ser** is used for unalterable qualities (**soy rubia**) and **estar** is used for variable qualities (**estoy triste**).

E. **Say if these sentences are right (✓) or wrong (X) according to their use of ser or estar. Example: Él es cansado X**

1. Teresa y Miguel son en el cine _____
2. Vosotros sois enfermos _____
3. La universidad está buena _____
4. Tú eres buen estudiante _____
5. Tú estás buena abogada _____
6. Yo estoy de Perú _____
7. Las flores son amarillas _____
8. Las sillas están de plástico _____
9. Susana está inteligente _____
10. Miguel y Juan son profesores _____
11. La moto está de Federico _____
12. Hoy está miércoles _____

F. **Now take the ones that are wrong and rewrite them with the right verb:**

_____

_____

_____

_____

_____

_____

6.2 Present Tense of Tener (*to have*)

Now that we're getting the hang of different verbs. Let's introduce another one! **Tener** is an extremely useful verb to know as it indicates that you possess something. In English this would mean 'to have.'

tener *to have*			
yo	**tengo**	nosotros/as	**tenemos**
tú	**tienes**	vosotros/as	**tenéis**
usted		ustedes	
él	**tiene**	ellos	**tienen**
ella		ellas	

> **Tip:** The **yo** form of tener is irregular. It should be "**teno**", but it's **tengo**. In other forms, the stem vowel **e** becomes **ie**: **tienes**.

Listen to a Song

How do you feel about listening to a song while practicing the verb **tener**? This song belongs to David Rodrígez Labault, a Latin Grammy-winning Puerto Rican singer, whose stage name is Siete (Seven). https://youtu.be/Cij71bcdr1l

These are the lyrics to his song. Try listening to it first, reading the words, and after you understand it, try singing it while you listen to it again. We know there are a lot of new words, but don't worry. This will help you train your ear and start to recognize new sounds.

No **tengo** un celular con diamantes	(I don't have a diamond-studded cellphone)
De muchos quilates pa' impresionar	(full of carats to impress others)
Pero **tengo** una buena conversación	(But I have good conversation)
Con la que te enamoro más y más	(to make you fall more in love with me.)
No **tengo** un jet privado	(I don't have a private jet)
Que compré con la Black Card	(that I bought with the Black Card)
Pero **tengo** una guagua vieja	(but I have an old van)
Con la que siempre vamos a pasear	(that we always go on a ride on.)
No **tengo** ropa de Versace	(I don't have Versace clothes)
Ni musculatura dura pa' enseñar	(nor hard muscles to show off)

Pero **tengo** un par de brazos desnudos	*(but I have a pair of bare arms)*
Que muy fuerte te van abrazar	*(that will embrace you really tight.)*
No soy como Mariah Carey	*(I'm not like Mariah Carey)*
Con un jacuzzi lleno de agua Evian	*(with a jacuzzi full of Evian water.)*
Pero **tengo** una chocita en la playa	*(But I have a little hut on the beach,)*
Pa' que te bañes con agüita de mar	*(so you can bathe in sea water.)*
Ricky **tiene** cara linda	*(Ricky has a cute face,)*
Enrique Iglesias los millones	*(Enrique Iglesias, the millions,)*
Y Aventura las mansiones	*(And Aventura, the mansions,)*
Pero...	*(But)*
Yo **tengo** tu amor	*(I have your love)*
I got your love	*(I got your love)*
Yo **tengo** tu amor	*(I have your love)*
Yo **tengo** tu love, yeah	*(I have your love, yeah)*
Yo **tengo** tu amor	*(I have your love)*
I got your love	*(I got your love)*
Yo **tengo** tu amor	*(I have your love)*
Yo **tengo** tu love, yeah	*(I have your love, yeah)*

Speak Abroad
Academy

Mucho and Poco

You can also describe nouns by saying something about their quantity. In English, we might say something like 'many dogs' or 'a few dogs.' There are words for these descriptors in Spanish, too. Unlike regular adjectives, they go *before* the noun instead of after.

Mucho/a/os/as *(a lot, many)*
This word must agree in gender and plurality with the noun they're in front of.
E.g. **Tengo muchos perros** (I have many dogs).

Mucho can also be an adverb, and remains invariable. Adverbs are words that describe verbs: **lee mucho** (*he reads a lot*).

Poco/a/os/as *(little, few, not many)*
This word also must agree in gender and plurality with the noun, too! E.g. **Tengo pocos vestidos** (*I have few dresses*).

Poco can also be an adverb, which means that it describes a verb, not just a noun. E.g. **Martín come poco** (*Martín doesn't eat much*).

Let's make it real! Time for some practical exercises to solidify your skills.

6.2. Practice

Complete the sentences with the correct form of **tener**.

Example: **Vosotros** _____ **muchas fiestas → Vosotros tenéis muchas fiestas.**

1. Nosotros _____ una casa muy linda.
2. Sofía y Pablo _____ seis televisiones.
3. Tú y Sara _____ muchos libros.
4. La abuela _____ pocos problemas.
5. Yo _____ dos manos.
6. El cine _____ muchos asientos.
7. Aquel jardín _____ muchos árboles.
8. Roberto y yo _____ un restaurante.
9. Tú _____ un jardín muy hermoso.
10. Ese museo _____ muchos cuadros interesantes.

Tener to Express Age

In Spanish, we use the verb **tener** (*to have*) to say how old we are. Instead of saying you *are of* a certain age, you say that you *have* a certain number of years.

I am [number] years old = Tengo [number] años.

In Spanish, you cannot omit the word **años** in this expression.

As for numbers, we'll dive into them more extensively in the next chapter! But for now, here are some translations of sentences expressing age:

I am thirty years old	**Tengo treinta años**
You are twenty-three years old	**Tienes veintitrés años**
He/she is forty years old	**Tiene cuarenta años**
We are fifteen years old	**Tenemos quince años**
You all are two years old	**Tenéis dos años**
They are eighteen years old	**Tienen dieciocho años**

> **Common Mistake:** Of course, English speakers tend to translate the structure they use in English directly into Spanish. This doesn't always work! In Spanish, you never use the verbs **ser** (*to be*) or **estar** (*to be*) to talk about age. You use the verb **tener**.
>
> Don't say: **Yo soy veinte años.** X
>
> Don't say: **Yo estoy veinte años.** X
>
> The right way to say it is: Yo tengo veinte años. ✓

Time to roll up your sleeves and practice!

B. Write the correct form of **tener** to convey these people's ages:

1. Manuel y José _____ veintiún años.
2. Yo _____ cincuenta años.
3. Tú _____ dieciocho años.
4. Marina y yo _____ treinta años.
5. Vosotros _____ veinticinco años.
6. Mi abuelo _____ setenta años.
7. Mi abuela _____ sesenta y cinco años.
8. Ellas _____ cuarenta y dos años.

C. Indicate if these sentences are right (✓) or wrong (X). Remember, to express age in Spanish you use the verb tener, not ser or estar like in English.

Example: X Él está veinte años.
                ✓ Él tiene veinte años.

1. Nosotros somos sesenta años. _____
2. Ustedes están cuarenta años. _____
3. Yo tengo cincuenta y dos años. _____
4. José y Daniel tienen treinta y cinco años. _____
5. Tú eres quince años. _____
6. María está seis años. _____
7. Tú y Miguel sois setenta años. _____
8. Josefina está veintitrés años. _____

D. Now take the ones that were wrong and rewrite them with the correct verb:

_____

_____

_____

_____

_____

E. Complete the following sentences using the correct verb form of **tener**.

1. Yo _____ muchos zapatos.
2. Nosotros _____ muchos amigos.
3. Marcos _____ un libro.
4. Tú _____ muchos gatos.
5. Vosotros _____ una abuela buena.
6. Ella _____ un lápiz rojo.
7. Carlos y María _____ una hija.
8. Usted _____ un sistema excelente.
9. Laura _____ 32 años.

CHAPTER 7:

NUMBERS

ONE, TWO, BUCKLE MY SHOE

If we're going to express the quantity of something, we obviously need to know our numbers. Just like in English, they're also essential for telling the date and time!

7.1 Numbers

#	English	Spanish	Pronunciation
0	zero	**cero**	*[theh-roh]*
1	one	**uno**	*[oo-noh]*
2	two	**dos**	*[dohs]*
3	three	**tres**	*[trehs]*
4	four	**cuatro**	*[kwah-troh]*
5	five	**cinco**	*[theen-koh]*
6	six	**seis**	*[seys]*
7	seven	**siete**	*[syeh-teh]*
8	eight	**ocho**	*[oh-choh]*
9	nine	**nueve**	*[nweh-beh]*
10	ten	**diez**	*[dyehth]*
11	eleven	**once**	*[ohn-theh]*
12	twelve	**doce**	*[doh-theh]*
13	thirteen	**trece**	*[treh-theh]*
14	fourteen	**catorce**	*[kah-tohr-theh]*
15	fifteen	**quince**	*[keen-theh]*
16	sixteen	**dieciséis**	*[dyeh-thee-seys]*
17	seventeen	**diecisiete**	*[dyeh-thee-syeh-teh]*
18	eighteen	**dieciocho**	*[dyeh-thee-oh-choh]*
19	nineteen	**diecinueve**	*[dyeh-thee-nweh-beh]*
20	twenty	**veinte**	*[beyn-teh]*

Ready to play with words? Let's practice!

7.1. Practice

Complete with **Uno, Una,** or **Un** according to each sentence.

Example: _____ perro → **Un perro.**

1. Tiene _____ año.
2. Tiene _____ lápiz.
3. Tenemos _____ gata.
4. _____, dos, tres, cuatro.
5. _____ hombre está caminando (*a man is walking*).
6. _____ flor amarilla.

7.2 There Is and There Are: *Hay*

Statements with hay

The word **hay** (pronounced like the English *eye*) means 'there is' and 'there are.' As you know, it's a useful way of describing the contents or arrangement of something. You can also use **hay** to turn something into a sentence by essentially saying 'is there?' or 'are there?'

You'll be relieved to know that **hay** is used for both singular and plural nouns. Whether you're talking about one cat in the house or more than one cat in the house, you would still use **hay** in either case.

Hay un gato en la casa (singular)

Hay gatos en la casa (plural)

Common Mistake: Don't use the Spanish definite articles **el, la, los,** and **las** (*the*) after **hay**. Use, instead, the definite articles after **hay**: **un, unos, una, unas.**

Don't say: **Hay el lápiz en la mesa.** X

Say: **Hay un lápiz en la mesa** (*there is a pencil on the table*) ✓

Tip: When **hay** is followed by a plural noun, you don't need the article:

Don't say: **Hay las flores en el jardín**. X

Say: **Hay flores en el jardín.** ✓

English	Spanish
There are fifteen dogs in the street	**Hay quince perros en la calle**
There is one person in the office	**Hay una persona en la oficina**
There is a tree in the yard	**Hay un árbol en el jardín**
There is a lot of food in the supermarket	**Hay mucha comida en el supermercado**
There are two German tourists on the train	**Hay dos turistas alemanes en el tren**

Get your learning hat on; it's time for some hands-on practice!

7.2. Practice

A. Look at these sentences and decide if you should leave them as they are (write a check mark next to them) or if they need to be changed. In that case, write the correct sentence next to them.

Example: **Hay un gato en el jardín** ✓

   1. Hay la alfombra en la casa._____
   2. Hay los tigres en el zoológico._____
   3. Hay manzanas en la verdulería._____
   4. Hay un cuadro en el museo._____
   5. Hay las oficinas en el edificio._____
   6. Hay muchos niños en el colegio. _____
   7. Hay los turistas en la ciudad._____
   8. Hay las personas en el cine. _____

The Negative with Hay

To make a sentence negative, just add a **no** before **hay**:

No hay quince perros en la calle. → *There are not fifteen dogs in the street.*

No hay dos turistas alemanes en el tren. →*There are not two German tourists on the train.*

The Interrogative With Hay

To ask a question with **hay**, follow the same order as with the statement, but add a question mark at the beginning and the end of the sentence, as all Spanish interrogative sentences are. If you're speaking this sentence out loud, you can use the tone of your voice to indicate that you're asking a question, just like you do in English. With a simple rising intonation, you can convey that you're asking a question, not making a statement.

English	Spanish + Pronunciation
Are there two dogs in the street?	**¿Hay dos perros en la calle?** *[eye dohs peh-rrohs ehn lah kah-yeh]*
Is there one person in the office?	**¿Hay una persona en la oficina?** *[eye uhnah pehr-soh-nah ehn lah oh-fee-thee-nah]*
Is there a tree in the yard?	**¿Hay un árbol en el jardín?** *[eye uhn ahr-bohl ehn ehl hahr-deen]*
Is there a lot of food in the supermarket?	**¿Hay mucha comida en el supermercado?** *[eye moo-chah koh-mee-dah ehn ehl soo-pehr-mehr-kah-doh]*
Are there two German tourists on the train?	**¿Hay dos turistas alemanes en el tren?** *[eye dohs too-rees-tahs ah-leh-mahn ehn ehl trehn]*

Difference between **hay** and **estar**.

Use **hay** (there is/there are) when you're talking about the existence of something/someone. For example, **hay un museo en mi ciudad** (*There is a museum in my city*).

Use **estar**, which means 'to be,' when you're talking about where something or someone *is*. For example, **el colegio está en la esquina** (*The school is on the corner*).

Ready to apply what you've learned? Let's practice!

B.   Translate the following to English:

Example: ¿Hay lápices en tu casa? Are there pencils in your house?

1.   ¿Hay flores en el jardín? _____
2.   ¿Hay sillas en la oficina? _____
3.   ¿Hay gatos en la calle? _____
4.   ¿Hay hoteles en la ciudad? _____
5.   ¿Hay una televisión en la casa? _____
6.   ¿Hay doctores en el hospital? _____
7.   ¿Hay un perro en el coche? _____
8.   ¿Hay una radio en el coche? _____
9.   ¿Hay dos mujeres en la pescadería?_____
10.   ¿Hay mesas en un restaurante? _____

C.   **Turn these affirmative sentences into negative sentences. Place no before hay.**

1.   Hay animales en el zoológico: _____
2.   Hay muchos niños en el parque: _____
3.   Hay un teléfono público en la calle: _____

4. Hay mucha gente en el restaurante: _____

5. Hay un buen hotel en la ciudad: _____

6. Hay muchos planetas en el cielo: _____

D. Fill in the blanks with hay or está:

1. ¿Dónde _____ el correo?

2. En el colegio _____ un gran parque.

3. La iglesia _____ en la esquina.

4. La universidad _____ junto al parque.

5. _____ restaurantes muy buenos en mi ciudad.

6. En la plaza central _____ dos bares.

7. ¿_____ un parque allá?

8. Sí, el parque _____ allá.

9. ¿Dónde_____ el parque?

10. _____ un parque cerca.

7.3 *To do | To make*: hacer

Let's learn some more verbs. **Hacer** is a useful verb that allows you to say, 'to do' or 'to make.' It's helpful when we're talking about activities!

Hacer is an irregular verb like some of the others we've covered, which means that it looks different depending on the pronouns that are next to it.

hacer *to do/to make*			
yo	**hago**	nosotros/as	**hacemos**
tú	**haces**	vosotros/as	**hacéis**
usted		ustedes	
él	**hace**	ellos	**hacen**
ella		ellas	

Hacer can also be used to talk about the weather in an impersonal way. In this case, we use it as a third-person verb, just like we would use it for the pronouns for 'he' or 'she.' It looks like this...

It's cold: **hace frío**   *It's windy*: **hace viento**

It's hot: **hace calor**   *It's sunny*: **hace sol**

Vocabulary: the weather

Nubes: clouds   →   hay nubes/está nublado

Lluvia: rain   →   hay lluvia/está lloviendo/llueve

Nieve: snow   →   hay nieve /está nevando/nieva

Viento: wind   →   hay viento /está ventoso/ventea

Let's spice things up with a practical exercise—time to practice!

7.3. Practice

Say what the weather is like according to what people are wearing/ doing.

1. Maria is wearing shorts and a T-shirt: _____
2. Tomás is wearing a scarf, gloves, and a jacket: _____
3. Luis is wearing a windbreaker: _____
4. Teresa is wearing sunblock: _____
5. Paula is wearing a raincoat: _____
6. Guillermo is looking at the snow through the window: _____
7. Carlos is looking at the clouds in the sky: _____

Vocabulary: Everyday Objects

English	Spanish	Pronunciation
the suitcase	la maleta	[lah mah-leh-tah]
the exercise	el ejercicio	[ehl eh-hehr-thee-thyoh]
the homework	la tarea	[lah tah-reh-ah]
the yoga	el yoga	[ehl yow-gah]
the sports	el deporte	[ehl deh-pohr-teh]
the swimming	la natación	[lah nah-tah-thyohn]
the breakfast	el desayuno	[ehl dehs-ah-yoo-noh]
the lunch	el almuerzo	[ehl ahl-mwehr-thoh]
the teatime	el té	[ehl teh]
the dinner	la cena	[lah theh-nah]

B. **Use the appropriate form of hacer (*to do/to make*) in these sentences:**

1. Nosotros _____ las maletas (*suitcases*).
2. Juan e Isabel _____ un pastel.
3. Yo _____ ejercicio (*exercise*)
4. Los niños _____ la tarea (*homework*)
5. _____ calor.
6. Mi hermana _____ yoga.
7. Tú _____ deporte.
8. Vosotros _____ natación.
9. _____ mucho frío.

7.4 The Interrogative ¿Cuánto/a? ¿Cuántos/as?

Questions are important! How else can we discover information from other people? Let's start off with some of the most important interrogative words for everyday life.

➲ **¿Cuánto/a?** *How much?*　　　➲ **¿Cuántos/as?** *How many?*

In English, 'much' is used for nouns that are uncountable, whereas 'many' is for nouns that *are* countable. It's the same in Spanish!

When you're asking someone how much coffee they want, you're expecting a reply like 'a lot' or 'not that much,' which is uncountable. However, if you were to phrase it as how *many* coffees they want, you're expecting a countable response like 'two cups' or 'just one.'

Keep this same rule in mind when determining whether to use **cuánto/a** (not countable) or **cuántos/as** (countable).

Put on your linguistic explorer hat—it's expedition time into the realm of practice!

7.4. Practice

A. **Fill in the blanks with the right form of cuánto/a or cuántos/as.**

1. ¿_____ perros tiene usted?
2. ¿_____ comida hay en el supermercado?
3. ¿_____ gatos hay en el parque?
4. ¿_____ flores hay en el jardín?
5. ¿_____ idiomas hablas (*speak*)?
6. ¿_____ café hay?

B. Now we're going to tie in ¿cuántos? with hay. Answer the following questions using the written number.

Example: ¿**Cuántos** sofás **hay** en tu casa? **Hay** dos sofás en mi casa.

1. ¿Cuántos días hay en una semana (*week*)? _____
2. ¿Cuántas semanas (*weeks*) hay en un mes (*month*)? _____
3. ¿Cuántos días hay en un año (*year*)? _____
4. ¿Cuántos días hay en un fin de semana (*weekend*)?_____
5. ¿Cuántos días hay en el mes de febrero (*February*)? _____
6. ¿Cuántos dedos (*fingers*) hay en tu (*your*) mano? _____
7. ¿Cuántos hospitales hay en tu (*your*) ciudad? _____
8. ¿Cuántas televisiones hay en tu (*your*) casa? _____
9. ¿Cuántos árboles hay en tu (*your*) jardín? _____
10. ¿Cuántas sillas hay en tu casa? _____

C. Write sentences with the words that are suggested. Modify the words as needed to match the numbers and add articles when necessary.

Example: Hay/ tres/elefante/en/zoológico: Hay tres elefantes en el zoológico.

1. hay/dos/universidad/en/ciudad _____
2. hay/veinte/manzana/en/canasta (*basket*)_____
3. hay/doce/mes/en/año _____
4. hay/un/Estatua de la Libertad/en/Nueva York _____
5. hay/dos/ojo/en/cara _____
6. hay/mucho/edificio/en/ciudad_____

Speak Abroad
Academy

CHAPTER 8:

SABER AND CONOCER

TO KNOW IS KNOWING YOU KNOW NOTHING

8.1 To Know: *Saber*

The verb **saber** means 'to know' in English. However, just like some of the verbs we've discussed in prior chapters, it's not the only Spanish verb that has this meaning! **Saber** refers to a very specific type of knowledge. It's only used when we're talking about knowing facts, information, and skills. It *can't* be used when talking about knowing people, places, or things.

When *know* refers to *knowing facts* and *learned skills*, use **saber**.

For example, **sé matemáticas** *(I know mathematics)* or **sé nadar** *(I know how to swim)*.

saber *to know*			
yo	**sé**	nosotros/as	**sabemos**
tú	**sabes**	vosotros/as	**sabéis**
usted		ustedes	
él	**sabe**	ellos	**saben**
ella		ellas	

Saber is an irregular verb. But the only irregularity is with **sé**, which is used when talking about yourself in singular form. Normally, with verbs that end in -*er*, you would knock off the *er*, and add an *o* (**sabo** X). But with **saber**, it's just **sé** if you're talking only about yourself.

For example:

Yo sé (I know). **No sé** (I don't know).

> **Tip:** The first person singular of **saber** is **sé** with an accent. Be careful, because there is another word in Spanish that looks the same, but it doesn't have an accent: the **se** for reflexive verbs—**se lava** (pronoun)

Theory's backstage; it's showtime for practice! Get ready to shine in the language spotlight.

8.1. Practice

Write the appropriate form of the verb **saber** in each sentence.

1. Nosotros _____ español.
2. Tú _____ el teléfono de Luis.
3. Vosotros _____ la verdad.
4. ¿Elena _____ ese poema?
5. Yo _____ francés (*French*).
6. María _____ la lección.
7. Pedro y José _____ alemán(*German*).
8. Él _____ bailar el vals (*dance the waltz*)

8.2 To Know: *Conocer*

The other word for 'to know' is **conocer**. Unlike **saber,** you would use **conocer** when talking about knowing certain people or things.

When *know* refers to *being familiar or being acquainted with something or someone*, use **conocer**. For example, **conozco a Luis** (*I know Luis*).

conocer *to be familiar with* **or** *to meet*			
yo	**conozco**	nosotros/as	**conocemos**
tú	**conoces**	vosotros/as	**conocéis**
usted		ustedes	
él	**conoce**	ellos	**conocen**
ella		ellas	

Conocer is also an irregular verb. Here, too, the only irregularity is for the singular form of the first-person pronoun. Normally, with verbs that end in -*er*, you would knock off the *er*, and add an *o* (**conoco** X). But with **conocer**, you knock off the **cer** and add **zco**.

For example:

Yo conozco (*I know*). **No conozco** (*I don't know*). Every other person is the same as a regular -*er* verb: *tú conoces, él conoce, nosotros conocemos*, and so on.

The journey continues! Time to dive into the sea of practice, where each wave carries a lesson.

8.2. Practice

A. Write the appropriate form of the verb **conocer** in each sentence.
   1. Elena y Pedro _____ a la profesora.
   2. Juan _____ al doctor Pérez.
   3. Vosotros _____ el sistema.
   4. Nosotros _____ la comida francesa.
   5. Yo _____ la casa.
   6. María _____ la ciudad.
   7. Tú _____ el Louvre.
   8. Él _____ al turista.

B. Now let's see if you can tell when to use **saber** and when to use **conocer**. Choose one of the two and conjugate it to make it fit in the sentence: **Example: María _____ (conocer/saber) inglés → María sabe inglés.**
   1. Tomás _____ (conocer/saber) el sur de España.
   2. Vosotros _____ (conocer/saber) contar hasta diez en alemán.
   3. Elena y Pablo _____ (conocer/saber) jugar al golf.
   4. Él no _____ (conocer/saber) si hace frío.
   5. María _____ (conocer/saber) esa avenida.
   6. Tú _____ (conocer/saber) esa historia.
   7. Yo _____ (conocer/saber) dónde vive Jorge (*where Jorge lives*).
   8. Tú y Sara _____ (conocer/saber) las reglas del Monopoly.

C. Here, you are required to choose the right verb and conjugate it. You do not need to use the pronoun; it's just a cue to tell you how to conjugate the verb.
   1. _____ (yo/conocer/saber) a Matías.
   2. No _____ (nosotros/conocer/saber) dónde está el gato.
   3. _____ (vosotros/conocer/saber) muy bien las obras de Albéniz.
   4. Mi hermana no _____ (conocer/sabe) ese grupo musical (*band*).
   5. ¿_____ (tú/saber/conocer) a qué hora empieza (*starts*) la película?
   6. Mis primos _____ (saber/conocer) cinco idiomas.
   7. _____ (yo/conocer/saber) Brasil muy bien.
   8. ¿_____ (él/conocer/saber) a tu novio (*boyfriend*)?
   9. Isabel y Luisa _____ (conocer/saber) la lección muy bien.

> **Tip**: When you're talking about knowing a person, in Spanish you add **a** before the person: **Conoce a María.**

Speak Abroad
Academy

D. Decide if you should add an a after the verb conocer, depending on if what is known is a person or something else. Write the a in case it's needed or an X when you don't need it.
Example: Tú conoces _____ Pedro → Tú conoces *a* Pedro.

1. Julia conoce _____ Italia.
2. Conozco _____ una profesora que sabe seis idiomas.
3. Conocemos _____ el camino al restaurante.
4. Conocéis _____ muchos países del mundo.
5. Mi padre conoce _____ mi novio (*boyfriend*).
6. ¿Conoces _____ Luis?
7. Tú y Patricia conocéis _____ la señorita Martí.

8.3 Saber + Infinitive: To know how to do something

We've mentioned a lot of infinitive verbs so far. In fact, **saber** itself is an infinitive verb. It's the root word of every word, which means "to know "or "to play." When you use **saber** before an infinitive verb, you're saying that you *know* how to do something.

Sé hablar francés (*I know how to speak French*).

Here are some verbs and specific activities in the infinitive form that you can combine with **saber** to express your knowledge of a certain ability. Like, for example, **sabe nadar** (*he knows how to swim*), **sabe hablar español** (*he knows how to speak Spanish*).

Which of the following do you know how to do?

English	Spanish	Pronunciation
to swim	**nadar**	[nah-dahr]
to dance	**bailar**	[bay-lahr]
to sing	**cantar**	[khan-tahr]
to do artistic gymnastics	**hacer gimnasia artística**	[ha-ther heem-nah-syah ahr-tees-tee-kah]
to play tennis	**jugar al tenis**	[hoo-gahr ahl teh-nees]
to play the piano	**tocar el piano**	[toh-kahr ehl pyah-noh]
to play golf	**jugar al golf**	[hoo-gahr ahl golf]
to play football	**jugar al fútbol**	[hoo-gahr ahl foot-bohl]
to play basketball	**jugar al baloncesto**	[hoo-gahr ahl bah-lohn-thehs-toh]
to write novels	**escribir novelas**	[ehs-kree-beer noh-beh-lahs]
to speak	**hablar**	[ah-blahr]
to act	**actuar**	[ahk-twahr]

Theory's recess time; the spotlight is on you in the grand theater of language practice!

8.3. Practice

A. What do these people know how to do? Use the verb saber + the right infinitive and direct object to complete the sentences.

Example: Serena Williams sabe jugar al tenis.

1. Novak Djokovic _____
2. LeBron James _____
3. Tiger Woods _____
4. J. K. Rowling _____
5. Lionel Messi y Cristiano Ronaldo _____
6. Taylor Swift _____
7. Michael Phelps _____
8. Shakira _____
9. Meryl Streep _____
10. Simon Biles _____

B. Who do these famous people know? Write the appropriate sentence, picking a person from the right row and finding the correct match on the left. Remember to add the a after **conocer (conocer a + person). Example: El señor Increíble conoce a Elastigirl.**

Sherlock Holmes	Adán
Ashton Kutcher	Victoria Beckham
Rhett Butler	Hailey Bieber
Chris Martin	Watson
David Beckham	Dakota Johnson
Justin Bieber	Scarlett O'Hara
Eva	Mila Kunis

1. _____
2. _____
3. _____
4. _____
5. _____
6. _____
7. _____

C. Write a sentence following the cues given:

Example: (conocer)_____. (Laura/la tía Julia) → Laura conoce a la tía Julia

1. (conocer)_____ (yo/el profesor Blanco)
2. (conocer) _____ (mi hermana y yo/la madre de Juan)
3. (conocer)_____ (María y Luis/Sergio)
4. (conocer) _____(vosotros/director del área comercial)
5. (conocer) _____ (tú/tía Julia)
6. (conocer) _____ (Carlos/la tía Julia)
7. (conocer) _____ (Martín y Elena/la tía Julia)

D. Translate using saber or conocer depending on the context. Remember:

Conocer = to be familiar with something or someone.

Saber = to know facts and learned skills.

1. I know the truth _____
2. She knows Maria _____
3. They know how to swim _____
4. Pedro and Elena know New York _____
5. We know the answer _____
6. We know the student_____
7. You know my name _____
8. He knows the truth _____
9. The dog knows Juan _____
10. I know how to play the piano_____
11. We know the university _____

E. Saber or Conocer? Choose the right verb to complete the sentence.

1. María no _____ (sabe/conoce) nadar todavía (*yet*).
2. No _____ sé/conozco) esta computadora.
3. ¿_____ (sabes/conoces) Australia?
4. ¿_____ (conocen/saben) el teléfono de Luis?
5. Carlos no _____ (conoce/sabe) al doctor.

CHAPTER 9:

THE INDICATIVE MOOD:
PRESENT TENSE OF HABLAR (TO SPEAK) –
COMER (TO EAT) – VIVIR (TO LIVE)
SPEAKING OF WHICH

Verbs in Spanish ending in **-ar, -er,** and **-ir** are called *regular verbs* because they all follow a regular pattern. As we've discussed, Spanish verbs change according to the person and the number of the subject. They're much simpler to modify when we're dealing with regular verbs!

9.1 Verbs Ending in -ar

The -ar verbs follow the pattern of **hablar.** Below are some of them:

English	Spanish	Pronunciation
to work	**trabajar**	*[trah-bah-hahr]*
to study	**estudiar**	*[ehs-too-dyahr]*
to look	**mirar**	*[mee-rahr]*
to arrive	**llegar**	*[yeh-gahr]*
to look for	**buscar**	*[boos-kahrr]*
to teach	**enseñar**	*[ehn-seh-nyar]*
to buy	**comprar**	*[kohm-prahr]*
to need	**necesitar**	*[neh-theh-see-tahr]*
to pay	**pagar**	*[pah-gahr]*
to return (to a place)	**regresar**	*[rreh-greh-sahr]*
to take/to drink	**tomar**	*[toh-mahr]*
to prepare	**preparar**	*[preh-pah-rahr]*
to fix	**arreglar**	*[ah-rreh-glahr]*
to travel	**viajar**	*[biah-hahr]*
to explain	**explicar**	*[ehks-plee-kahr]*

Speak Abroad
Academy

The present ted by removing the infinitive **-ar** ending and replacing it with an ending corresponding to the person that is performing the action of the verb. See below:

hablar *to speak*			
yo	**habl-o**	nosotros/as	**habl-amos**
tú	**habla-s**	vosotros/as	**habl-áis**
usted		ustedes	
él	**habl-a**	ellos	**habl-an**
ella		ellas	

Ready to apply what you know? Let's practice!

9.1. Practice

A.   Check this dialogue. Can you translate what Luisa, and the grocer are saying?

En la verdulería

LUISA: Buenos días, ¿tiene bananas?

VERDULERO: Buenos días. Sí, tengo bananas.

LUISA: Ah, ¿cuánto cuesta?

VERDULERO: Cuesta 20 pesos el kilo.

LUISA: Muy bien. Necesito comprar dos kilos.

VERDULERO: Está bien. Aquí tiene.

LUISA: Muchas gracias. Adiós.

Glossary:

Tener: *to have*

¿Cuánto cuesta...?: *how much are...?*

Kilo: *kilogram*

Aquí tiene: *Here you are*

Vocabulary: The House

Here are some helpful vocabulary words that you'll need to know. They all refer to various parts of the house and some common items that you'll find in them.

English	Spanish	Pronunciation
the living room	la sala	[lah sah-lah]
the dining room	el comedor	[ehl koh-meh-dohr]
the kitchen	la cocina	[lah koh-thee-nah]
the cup	la taza	[lah tah-thah]
the glass	el vaso	[ehl bah-soh]
the refrigerator	el refrigerador	[ehl rreh-free-heh-rah-dohr]
the oven	el horno	[ehl ohr-noh]
the bedroom	la habitación	[lah ah-bee-tah-thyohn]
the garage	el garaje	[ehl gah-rah-heh]
the stairs	las escaleras	[lahs ehs-kah-leh-rahs]
the bathroom	el baño	[ehl bah-nyoh]
the mirror	el espejo	[ehl ehs-peh-hoh]
the roof	el techo	[ehl teh-choh]

B.   **Give the corresponding subject pronouns.**

Example: **regresáis <u>vosotros</u>**

1.   enseño _____
2.   cantamos _____
3.   estudian _____
4.   paga _____
5.   deseo_____

6.   buscas _____
7.   compra _____
8.   habláis _____
9.   trabajan _____
10.   regresas _____

C. En la biblioteca

Marcos está en la biblioteca. Estudia para un examen de matemáticas. El examen es mañana (*tomorrow*). Tiene muchos libros para leer. Marcos está preocupado. Necesita estudiar mucho. El examen es muy difícil.

Confirm whether these statements are true (**cierto**) or false (**falso**), based on the information in the paragraph above.

1. Marcos es un profesor _____
2. Marcos estudia en su (*his*) casa _____
3. Marcos tiene un examen mañana _____
4. El examen es muy fácil _____

D. Answer these questions of conjugating the verbs ending in -ar to match the person performing the action.

1. Mi padre _____(trabajar) de lunes a viernes.
2. Tus hijos _____(mirar) demasiada televisión.
3. Vosotros _____(buscar) buenos zapatos.
4. La profesora Oliva _____(enseñar) tres clases.
5. _____ (yo/comprar) frutas y verduras todas las semanas.
6. Teresa y Pedro _____(viajar) en tren al trabajo.
7. Nosotros les _____(explicar) a nuestros hijos cómo comportarse (*how to behave*).
8. El señor Romanelli _____(arreglar) carteras.

E. Fill in the blanks with the correct verb form:

Infinitive	hablar	enseñar	trabajar	mirar
yo		enseño		
tú	hablas			miras
él/ella/ usted			trabaja	
nosotros	hablamos			miramos
vosotros			trabajáis	
ellas/ellos/ ustedes		enseñan		

9.2 Verbs Ending in -er

The **-er** verbs follow the pattern of **comer**. Below are some of them:

English	Spanish	Pronunciation
to learn	**aprender**	*[ah-prehn-dehr]*
to eat	**comer**	*[koh-mehr]*
to drink	**beber**	*[beh-behr]*
to understand	**comprender**	*[kohm-prehn-dehr]*
to think to believe in	**creer (en)**	*[kreh-ehr]*
should, must, ought to (do something)	**deber (+ infinitivo)**	*[deh-behr]*
to read	**leer**	*[leh-ehr]*
to sell	**vender**	*[behn-dehr]*
to put in	**meter**	*[meh-tehr]*
to turn on	**prender**	*[prehn-dehr]*
to run	**correr**	*[koh-rrehr]*
to break	**romper**	*[rrohm-pehr]*

You'll notice that all these verbs end in **-er**! When we're speaking in the present tense, we remove the **-er** from verbs like the ones in the table above, and we add a new ending depending on the pronoun that goes before it. In other words, the ending of the word changes depending on who and how many people are being referred to.

Refer to the diagram box below for the rules on how to modify the endings of these verbs for each pronoun.

comer *to eat*			
yo	**com-o**	nosotros/as	**com-emos**
tú	**com-es**	vosotros/as	**com-éis**
usted		ustedes	
él	**com-e**	ellos	**co-men**
ella		ellas	

> **Tip: También** is an adverb. It means 'as well,' 'too,' or 'also.'

The indicative mood:

Speak Abroad
Academy

9.2. Practice

Reading Comprehension

En el restaurante

Estamos en el restaurante "Carlitos". Somos quince personas. Todos trabajamos juntos en la misma oficina. Tenemos una mesa grande. La carne de este restaurante es muy sabrosa. También hay pollo y pescado. Todo es sabroso. El camarero toma el pedido y regresa con la comida. Comemos y bebemos muy bien.

Glossary:

en: in	**carne**: meat	**pescado**: fish
todos: all	**de**: of	**todo**: everything
juntos: together	**este**: this	**camarero**: waiter
misma: the same	**también**: also	**pedido**: order
colegas: coworkers	**pollo**: chicken	**con**: with
muy bien: very well		

A. Answer the following questions in this text.

Example: ¿La carne de este restaurante es fea? No, la carne de este restaurante es sabrosa.

1. ¿Son veinte personas en la mesa? _____
2. ¿Todos trabajan en la misma oficina? _____
3. ¿Tienen pollo y pescado? _____
4. ¿Tienen una mesa pequeña? _____

B. Complete these sentences with the appropriate form of the right verb. Use each verb once.

beber - comprender - prender - leer - correr - comer - aprender - vender

1. El niño no _____ la lección.
2. Luis y María _____ la televisión.
3. La muchacha _____ al colegio para (to) no llegar tarde (late).
4. Nosotros _____ la casa.
5. Vosotros _____ en ese (that) restaurante excelente.
6. Tú y yo _____ mucha agua.
7. Todos los domingos _____ (yo) el periódico.
8. Todos los días _____ (tú) algo (something).

C. Fill in the blanks with the correct verb form:

Infinitive	comer	vender	creer	apender
yo	como			aprendo
tú		vendes		
él/ella/ usted			cree	
nosotros	comemos			aprendemos
vosotros		vendéis		
ellas/ellos/ ustedes			creen	

9.3 Verbs Ending in -ir

The **-ir** verbs follow the pattern of **vivir**. Below are some of them:

English	Spanish	Pronunciation
to open	abrir	[ah-breer]
to write	escribir	[ehs-kree-beer]
to receive	recibir	[rreh-thee-beer]
to share	compartir	[kohm-pahr-teer]
to decide	decidir	[deh-thee-deer]
to describe	describir	[dehs-kree-beer]
to discuss	discutir	[dees-koo-teer]
to go up	subir	[soo-beer]
to suffer	sufrir	[soo-freer]

We talked about how to modify verbs ending in **-er**, but what about verbs that end in **-ir**? To use these verbs in the present tense, we remove the **-ir** ending and change it according to the subject, just like the other verbs. See below for how to modify these verbs.

vivir *to live*			
yo	**vivo**	nosotros/as	**vivimos**
tú	**vives**	vosotros/as	**vivís**
usted		ustedes	
él	**vive**	ellos	**viven**
ella		ellas	

The indicative mood:

Speak Abroad
Academy

> **Tip:** In English, a verb must have an expressed subject (**he** eats spaghetti). In Spanish, 'he' or 'she' is not always necessary. Why? Because it's obvious from the verb who you are referring to. People tend to omit using subject pronouns unless you want to clarify who's doing the action or place emphasis on it.

> **Common Mistake:** You might feel it's natural to add a pronoun in Spanish but think twice before you do it. Most of the time, your verbs will do the work for you!
>
> **X** Don't say: **Yo quiero un café** (*I want a coffee*)
>
> ✓ Say instead: **Quiero un café**
>
> **X** Don't say: **Nosotros queremos ir a la playa mañana** (*We want to go to the beach tomorrow*)
>
> ✓ Say instead: **Queremos ir a la playa mañana**

Ready to play with words? Let's practice!

9.3. Practice

A. Complete these sentences with the appropriate form of the correct verbs listed. Use each verb once.

vivir - subir- escribir- recibir - discutir - decidir - compartir - abrir

1. Los niños _____ los caramelos (*candy*).
2. Todos los estudiantes _____ las escaleras para ir a (*to go to*) la clase de matemáticas.
3. Marcos _____ en la ciudad; María _____ en el campo (*country*)
4. Yo _____ la puerta (*door*).
5. Tú _____ a tus amigos en tu casa.
6. Vosotros _____ cartas (*letters*) a vuestros padres.
7. Nosotros _____ las noticias (*the news*) con mi marido (*husband*).
8. Tú _____ estudiar español.

B. Fill in the blanks with the correct verb form:

Infinitive	escribir	recibir	abrir	subir
yo	escribo			subo
tú		recibes		
él/ella/usted			abre	
nosotros	escribimos			subimos
vosotros		recibís		
ellas/ellos/ ustedes			abren	

CHAPTER 10:

WHAT TIME IS IT?

Navigating everyday life would be pretty hard without the ability to ask for and express the time. In this lesson, we'll go over everything you need to know to understand this crucial component of language.

10.1 What Time Is It?

To ask, 'what time is it?' in Spanish, you say **¿Qué hora es?** *[keh oh-rah ehs]*

If it's one o'clock, the response will be **Es la una.** *[ehs lah uhnah]*

And if it's a number higher than one, you'll phrase it as **son las dos** or **son las tres**, and so on. As you can see, we're using **es** again, which is both the singular and plural third-person form of the verb **ser**.

Es la una	*It's one o'clock*
Son las dos	*It's two o'clock*
Son las cuatro	*It's four o'clock*
Son las diez	*It's ten o'clock*

If you want to say "sharp" or "exactly," Spanish uses **exactamente** or **en punto**.

Son las once en punto	*It's eleven o'clock sharp*
Son las seis en punto	*It's six o'clock sharp*
Son las ocho en punto	*It's sharp eight o'clock*

If, instead, you're kind of hesitant about the time, you can say **más o menos** *(about)*.

Son las nueve más o menos	*It's about nine o'clock*
Es la una más o menos	*It's about one o'clock*

Speak Abroad
Academy

If you want to say it's half past the hour, use **y media** or **y treinta**. For example, **son las ocho y media** (*it's eight thirty*).

Son las doce y media	*It's twelve thirty*
Son las diez y treinta	*It's ten thirty*
Son las cuatro y media	*It's four thirty*

To indicate that it's a number past the hour, use **y + number of minutes**: For example, **son las siete y veinte** (it's 7:20).

Son las dos y cinco	*It's 2:05*
Son las seis y diez	*It's 6:10*
Son las ocho y veinte	*It's 8:20*
Es la una y veinticinco	*It's 1:25*

And to say it's a number to the hour, say **menos + number of minutes**. For example, **son las tres menos veinte** (it's twenty to three).

Son las nueve menos diez	*It's 8:50*
Es la una menos veinte	*It's 12:40*
Son las cuatro menos cinco	*It's 3:55*
Son las doce menos veinticinco	*It's 11:35*

What about fifteen minutes past the hour?

In Spanish, when it's a quarter after the hour, you say **y cuarto** (*quarter*) or **y quince** (*fifteen*).

| Son las siete y cuarto = It's 7:15 | Son las cuatro y cuarto = It's 4:15 | Son las seis y cuarto = It's 6:15 |

And when it's fifteen minutes before the hour, in Spanish you say **menos cuarto** or, less frequently, **menos quince**.

Son las ocho menos cuarto	*It's 7:45*
Son las tres menos cuarto	*It's 2:45*
Es la una menos cuarto	*It's 12:45*

Another way of expressing the time before the hour is saying the **number of minutes + para + la hora** (the hour). For example: **Son diez para las dos**.

Son veinte para las cuatro	*It's twenty minutes to four o'clock*
Son diez para la una	*It's ten minutes to one o'clock*
Son veinticinco para las doce	*It's twenty-five minutes to twelve o'clock*

Here are more examples:

Es la una

Son las once

Son las seis

Es la una menos diez

Son las ocho y media

Son las siete y veinte

Speak Abroad
Academy

Unleash the power of words! It's practice o'clock, where language mastery comes to life. Let's go!

10.1. Practice

A.

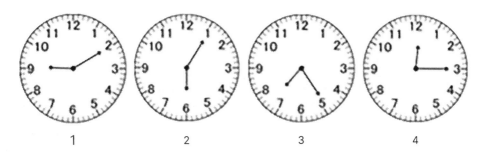

1   2   3   4

¿Qué hora es? State in words what time it is on each clock.

1. _____

2. _____

3. _____

4. _____

B. ¿Qué hora es?

1. 3:45: _____   4. 6:45: _____

2. 11:00: _____   5. 8:15: _____

3. 1:30: _____   6. 9:20: _____

C. State what time it is and what it's time for.

Example: 12:00 a.m. → Son las doce. Es hora de almorzar.

Some activities you might use are: **cenar** (*have dinner*) - **caminar - trabajar - mirar televisión - correr - regresar a casa - buscar a mis hijos** (*pick my kids up*) - **comer -**

1. 8:00 a.m.: _____   4. 4:30 p.m.: _____

2. 10:00 a.m.: _____   5. 6:00 p.m.: _____

3. 1:15 p.m.: _____   6. 8:00 p.m.: _____

D. At what time do we travel to... Form sentences according to the cues. Example: Londres / 8:15 → ¿A qué hora viajamos a Londres? A las ocho y cuarto.

1. París /12.00   4. Lima / 9:15

2. Madrid / 1:00   5. Buenos Aires / 8:45

3. Praga / 5:30   6. Washington / 5:45

10.2 At what time is...?

To indicate at what time something is happening, in Spanish you ask, "**¿A qué hora es...?**" ("*At what time is...?*"). And the answer is, "**A la/las...**" (*At...*) or "**Es a la /las...**" ("*It's at...*")

¿A qué hora es la comida?	*At what time is dinner?*
Es a la una.	*It's at one.*
¿A qué hora es el programa?	*At what time is the program?*
Es a las tres.	*It's at three.*

> **Tip**: Note that **comida** can mean *food*, but it can also mean *dinner* or the *moment you eat.*

What about references to the time of day? Spanish also specifies whether something happens in the morning, at noon, in the afternoon, or at night.

de la mañana	*of the morning: a.m.*
del mediodía	*of noon: p.m.*
de la tarde	*of the afternoon: p.m.*
de la noche	*of the night: p.m.*
de la medianoche	*of midnight: a.m.*
Es a las tres de la mañana	*It's at three in the morning (3:00 a.m.)*
Es a las ocho de la noche	*It's at eight in the evening (8:00 p.m.)*
Es a las doce del mediodía	*It's at twelve noon (12:00 p.m.)*
Es a las doce de la medianoche	*It's at twelve midnight (12:00 a.m.)*

Vocabulary: Social events

English	Spanish	Pronunciation
the party	**la fiesta**	*[lah fyehs-tah]*
the class	**la clase**	*[lah klah-seh]*
the meeting	**la reunión**	*[lah reyoo-nyohn]*
the lunch meeting	**el almuerzo**	*[ehl ahl-mwehr-thoh]*
the appointment	**la cita**	*[lah thee-tah]*
the event	**el evento**	*[ehl eh-behn-toh]*

Enough talk; let's do some practice!

10.2. Practice

In everyday language, you can omit the verb **es** when you're **answering** a time that something happens; for example, **¿A qué hora es la comida?** The answer would be **A las ocho de la noche.**

A. Respond to some more questions by spelling out the numbers and including the time indicated. You can add "de la mañana", "de la tarde", "de la medianoche" or "del mediodía" to make it more complete! Example: ¿A qué hora es la comida? <u>A las tres de la tarde.</u>

1. ¿A qué hora es el almuerzo? (12:00 p.m.)_____
2. ¿A qué hora es la cita? (4:00p.m.)_____
3. ¿A qué hora es tu clase? (8:00 a.m.)_____
4. ¿A qué hora es la reunión? (11:00 a.m.)_____
5. ¿A qué hora es la fiesta? (12:00a.m.)_____
6. ¿A qué hora es el evento? (3:00 p.m.)_____

B. Translate these expressions:

1. It's eleven o'clock sharp: _____
2. It's eight thirty: _____
3. It's eight in the morning: _____
4. It's about three o'clock in the afternoon: _____
5. It's ten thirty: _____
6. It's five thirty: _____
7. It's seven twenty: _____
8. It's twenty to one: _____
9. It's five to two: _____
10. It's twenty-five to two: _____
11. It's eight fifteen: _____
12. It's a quarter to four: _____

10.3 The Days of the Week

English	Spanish	Pronunciation
Monday	**lunes**	*[loo-nehs]*
Tuesday	**martes**	*[mahr-tehs]*
Wednesday	**miércoles**	*[meeehr-koh-lehs]*
Thursday	**jueves**	*[hweh-behs]*
Friday	**viernes**	*[byehr-nehs]*
Saturday	**sábado**	*[sah-bah-doh]*
Sunday	**domingo**	*[doh-meeng-goh]*

If you want to say you do something on a certain day every week, you say:
Trabajo los lunes. (*I work on Mondays*)

If you want to say you do something from one day to another, you say:
Trabajo de lunes a viernes. (*I work from Monday to Friday*)

If you want to say you do something on the weekends, you say:
Juego al tenis los fines de semana. (*I play tennis on the weekends*)

Mini-Challenge:

Listen to the song *Lunes otra vez* (*Monday, again*), by Argentine singer, songwriter, and musician Charlie García. It brings to mind the Monday blues, prevalent in every culture around the globe. Try to follow the lyrics while you do.

Lunes otra vez	Monday, again
Lunes otra vez sobre la ciudad. La gente que ves vive en soledad. Sobre el bosque gris veo morir al sol que mañana sobre la avenida nacerá.	*Monday again over the city.* *The people you see live in solitude.* *On the gray forest, I see the sun dying* *that tomorrow will shine again on the avenue.*
Calles sin color, vestidas de gris. Desde mi ventana veo el verde tapiz de una plaza que mañana morirá, y muerto el verde solo hierro crecerá	*Colorless roads, dressed in gray.* *From my window I see the green carpet* *of a park that will die tomorrow,* *and once the green dies, only iron will grow.*
Viejas en la esquina mendigan su pan; en las oficinas, muerte en sociedad. Todos ciegos hoy sin saber mirar la espantosa risa de la pálida ciudad.	*Old women in the corner beg for bread;* *in the offices, the death of society.* *Everyone is blind today, not knowing how to see* *the horrid laughter of the pale city.*
Lunes otra vez sobre la ciudad. La gente que ves vive en soledad. Siempre será igual, nunca cambiará. Lunes es el día triste y gris de soledad.	*Monday again over the city.* *The people you see live in solitude.* *It will always be the same, it will never change* *Monday is the sad and gray day of solitude.*

Speak Abroad
Academy

Time to roll up your sleeves and practice!

10.3. Practice

A. Answer these questions about the song *Lunes otra vez:*

1. ¿De qué color es el lunes para este autor? _____
2. ¿Cómo es el lunes? _____
3. ¿Cómo vive la gente? (*How do people live?*)_____
4. ¿Qué no saben hacer los ciegos (*blind people*)? _____

B. Look at Mónica's schedule and answer the questions below:

	LUNES	MARTES	MIÉRCOLES	JUEVES
9:15	pagar cuentas			tomar un café con Elena
10:30	estudiar	estudiar	estudiar	estudiar
11:45				
4:15	buscar niños colegio	buscar niños colegio	buscar niños colegio	buscar niños colegio
6:45	preparar comida	preparar comida	preparar comida	preparar comida
8:15	cenar	cenar	cenar	cenar

	VIERNES	SÁBADO	DOMINGO
9:15			
10:30	estudiar	jugar al tenis	jugar al golf
11:45			
4:15	buscar niños colegio		
6:45	preparar comida	restaurante	pedir pizza (*order pizza*)
8:15	cenar		

1. ¿A qué hora busca Mónica a los niños al colegio? _____
2. ¿A qué hora paga las cuentas? _____
3. ¿A qué hora estudia? _____
4. ¿Cuándo estudia? _____
5. ¿Cuándo juega al tenis? _____
6. ¿Cuándo juega al golf? _____

10.4 The Months of the Year

English	Spanish	Pronunciation
January	**enero**	[eh-neh-roh]
February	**febrero**	[feh-breh-roh]
March	**marzo**	[mahr-thoh]
April	**abril**	[ah-breel]
May	**mayo**	[may-yoh]
June	**junio**	[hoo-nyoh]
July	**julio**	[hoo-lyoh]
August	**agosto**	[ah-gohs-toh]
September	**septiembre**	[sehp-tyehm-breh]
October	**octubre**	[ohk-too-breh]
November	**noviembre**	[noh-byehm-breh]
December	**diciembre**	[dee-thyehm-breh]

> **Tip:** Now that we're learning about time, the adverb **¿cuándo?** (*when*) is a useful word to know.

Other period expressions:

¿Qué fecha es hoy?	*What is today's date?*
Hoy es 18 de agosto.	*Today is August 18.*
Hoy es el primero de mayo.	*Today is May 1st.*
Mi cumpleaños es el 2 de junio.	*My birthday is June 2.*
La fiesta es el 8 de octubre.	*The party is October 8.*

When it's the first day of the month, you should use the ordinal number **primero**. After that, cardinal numbers (**dos, tres, cuatro**, and so on) should be used.

> **Tip:** Remember to use the article **el** before the date when you're stating when an event takes place: **La reunión es el 7 de noviembre** (*the meeting is on November 7*).

> **Tip:** The months of the year and the days of the week are not capitalized in Spanish: **hoy es lunes, 2 de marzo.**

Common Error:

When you want to say, "Today is Thursday,"

X   Don't say: **Hoy es el jueves.**

✓   Say instead: **Hoy es jueves.** (omit the **el**)

Tip: On the other hand, if you want to state when a specific event takes place, always use **el**. For example:

Navidad es **el** 25 de diciembre

Año Nuevo es **el** primero de enero

Mi cumpleaños es **el** 4 de agosto

La independencia de Estados Unidos es **el** 4 de julio.

The year is divided into seasons: summer (verano), fall or autumn(otoño), winter (invierno), and spring (primavera).

el verano	**junio**	**el otoño**	**septiembre**
	julio		**octubre**
	agosto		**noviembre**
la primavera	**marzo**	**el invierno**	**diciembre**
	abril		**enero**
	mayo		**febrero**

Ready to play with words? Let's practice!

10.4. Practice

A.   State when these events take place:

1.   ¿Cuándo es tu cumpleaños (birthday)?

_____

2.   ¿Cuándo se celebra la independencia de Estados Unidos?

_____

3.   ¿Cuándo empieza (*starts*) el verano en Europa?

_____

4.   ¿Cuándo es Navidad (*Christmas*)?

_____

5.   ¿Cuándo es Año Nuevo (*New Year's*)?

_____

B. Link the words with the season of the year and write a sentence.

Example: **nieve → invierno. En invierno hay nieve** or **frío → invierno. En invierno hace frío.**

Seasons: primavera - verano - otoño - invierno

1. Flores → _____

2. Sol → _____

3. Hojas secas (*dry leaves*) → _____

4. Calor → _____

5. Viento → _____

6. Hielo (*ice*) → _____

CHAPTER 11:

AFFIRMATIVE AND NEGATIVE SENTENCES

YES, SIR; NO, SIR

Affirmative and negative sentences are an important part of everyday conversations. When we use an affirmative sentence, we're saying something *is* or that something *did* happen. It's a positive statement. On the other hand, negative sentences express that something is *not* or that something *didn't* happen. It's the opposite of an affirmative sentence.

An affirmative sentence would be 'the cat is blue.' In retort to this, a negative sentence would be 'the cat is not blue.'

So, how do we express these positive and negative sentences in Spanish?

11.1 Affirmative and Negative Sentences

We've covered a lot of affirmative sentences already in the book. But let's give you a refresher on how to write these sentences.

When constructing an affirmative sentence in Spanish, the subject (the noun) usually goes at the beginning of the sentence. After the noun, we add the verb. We end up with a sentence such as:

El perro salta *(The dog jumps)*

There are also words that, by default, are affirmative words.

In Spanish, they are:

• **algo**	*something*
• **alguien**	*someone*
• **algún, alguno, alguna**	*one, a, an, any*
• **algunos algunas**	*some, any*
• **a veces, algunas veces**	*sometimes*
• **siempre**	*always*
• **también**	*also / too / as well*

Let's go back to the sentence about the dog jumping. What if we wanted to turn this sentence into a negative one and state that the dog is *not* jumping?

To do so, we'd add the word **no** right after the noun and before the verb.

El perro no salta (*The dog does not jump*)

Just as there are affirmative words, there are also inherently negative words.

Negative words are:

• **no**	*no*	• **nunca**	*never*
• **ni**	*neither / nor*	• **ninguno**	*not one*
• **nada**	*nothing*	• **jamás**	*never*
• **nadie**	*no one / nobody*		

Do you know what a double negative is? We use them in English all the time. They're technically not grammatically correct to use in any language, but they're extremely common in everyday, informal speech.

A double negative sentence occurs when we combine two negative words in the same sentence. Like, for example, 'She didn't do nothing' or 'I didn't see nobody.' They're confusing because the technical meaning is different from their intended meaning. When someone says, 'She didn't do nothing' they *mean* to emphasize that 'She didn't do anything.'

To construct a double negative sentence in Spanish, you add a negative word before *and* after the main verb in a sentence. The first word is usually 'no.' For example:

Ella no tiene <u>nada</u>   (*She doesn't have nothing*)

In other words, it's arranged as subject + **no** + verb + **nada.**

Let's take a look at the following negative and double negative sentences:

La niña no come nada	*The girl doesn't eat nothing.*
No sé nada	*I know nothing.*
El niño no comprende nada	*The boy doesn't understand nothing.*
Luis no compra nada en la verdulería	*Luis buys nothing in the fruit store.* *Luis doesn't buy anything in the fruit store.*
Nosotros no necesitamos nada	*We need nothing.* *We don't need anything.*

> **Tip:** How do you translate a sentence like **The man doesn't speak Spanish**? Well, in Spanish there is no equivalent for the English word *do* or *does* in negative sentences. You simply say **El hombre no habla español.**

Speak Abroad
Academy

The negative words you use to form **double negative sentences** in Spanish are:

1. Adverbs of denial (see below)
2. Indefinite pronouns ('anything,' 'something,' etc.)

11.2 Adverbs of Denial

no	*no - not*
ni	*nor - neither*
nunca	*never*
tampoco	*neither*
jamás	*never, ever*

The order of words in the sentence es **no + verb + adverb of denial + complement**

Examples:

- **No** me gusta **ni** la natación ni el tenis: *I don't like swimming or tennis*
- Maria **no** come **ni** frutas ni verduras: *Maria doesn't eat vegetables or fruits*
- **No** voy **nunca** a un restaurante: *I never go to a restaurant*
- Luis **no** visita **nunca** a Elena: *Luis never visits Elena*

> **Careful!** You **don't** include the word **no** when a negative adverb shows up **before** the verb:
>
> - **Nadie está en la calle.** (*Nobody is on the street.*)
> - **Nunca veo a mi tía.** (*I never see my aunt.*)
> - **Miguel tampoco bebe café.** (Miguel doesn't drink coffee either.)

11.3 Indefinite Pronouns

The other way to create double negative sentences in Spanish is with **indefinite pronouns**. They're 'indefinite' because they're vague about who they are referring to, e.g., 'someone' or 'anyone.' They can also be negative like 'no one' or 'nothing.'

The order is the same as with adverbs of denial: **no + verb + indefinite pronoun + complement**

These are negative indefinite pronouns:

nadie	*no one / nobody*
nada	*nothing / anything*
ninguna, ninguno	*any / none / anyone / no one*

Examples:

- ⮑ **No** hay **nada** para comer en la casa: *There is nothing to eat in the house*
- ⮑ **No** comprendo **nada** en alemán: *I don't understand any German*
- ⮑ **No** necesita **ninguno**: *He/she doesn't need any of them*
- ⮑ **No** hay **nadie** en la ciudad: *There is no one in the city*

Practice makes perfect—let's give it a go!

11. Practice

Reading Comprehension: Check this dialogue out.

Teresa goes to her friend Isabel's dinner party, but she doesn't care for anything to eat.

Isabel:	¿Deseas **algo** para comer? *Do you want something to eat?*
Teresa:	**No**, gracias. **No** voy a comer **nada**. *No, thank you. I won't eat anything.*
Isabel:	¿Y algo para beber? *And something to drink?*
Teresa:	**Tampoco** beberé **nada**. *I won't drink anything either.*
Isabel:	¿**No** deseas **nada**, en serio? *You really don't want anything?*
Teresa:	**Nunca** ceno **nada**. *I never have anything for dinner.*
Isabel:	¿**Jamás** comes por la noche? *You never eat anything at night?*
Teresa:	**No**. Duermo mejor. *No. I sleep better.*

Speak Abroad
Academy

Notice that when the adverbs or pronouns of denial are placed directly **before** the first verb, you don't need the double negative: **Jamás comes por la noche.**

Ninguno/ninguna is an adjective. It must concur in number and gender with the noun it modifies: **No tiene ninguna habitación**.

When **ninguno** is before a masculine singular noun, it shortens to **ningún**.

Ninguno/a is not used in the plural unless it accompanies a noun that is always in the plural, like **vacaciones** (vacations): **No necesitan ningunas vacaciones.**

If **ninguno/a** precedes the noun, you don't need a **no: Ninguna persona comprende el latín.**

Remember: the opposite of **ninguno** (*no one*) is **alguno** (*someone / some*)

A. Answer these questions about the dialogue above:

1. ¿Teresa desea comer algo? _____
2. ¿Teresa desea beber algo? _____
3. ¿Teresa desea algo?_____
4. ¿Teresa cena alguna vez por la noche? _____

B. Give the opposite of the following:

1. algo _____
2. alguien _____
3. alguno _____
4. siempre _____
5. también _____

6. nada _____
7. nadie _____
8. ninguno _____
9. nunca _____
10. tampoco _____

C. Translate the following using **algún, alguno, alguna** (*one, a, an, any*), **algunos, algunas** (*some, any*), and **ningún, ninguno, ninguna** (*none, no one*).

Example: **Do you have any idea?** → **¿Tienes alguna idea?**

1. Do you have any fruit? _____
2. Do you have any sweaters? _____
3. I don't have any shirts. _____
4. Did you buy a blouse? _____
5. No, I didn't buy any blouses. _____
6. Are there some boys in the pool? _____
7. No, there aren't any boys in the pool. _____
8. Do you have any cats at home? _____
9. No, I don't have any cats at home_____
10. Do you have any suitcases in the car? _____
11. No, I don't have any suitcases in the car. _____

D. Eduardo walks into his house and looks around the place, trying to find his car keys. He searches inside his backpack and there is nothing there. In his room he finds his empty wallet, but not his keys. The dining table is empty, so Eduardo keeps searching. He even looks inside the refrigerator! He only finds a banana. After half an hour, Eduardo notices that there is something in his pocket; his keys.

Answer the questions.

Example: ¿Hay algo en el refrigerador? → **Sí, hay algo. No, no hay nada.**

1. ¿Hay algo en su mochila? _____
2. ¿Hay algo en el refrigerador? _____
3. ¿Hay algo en la mesa? _____
4. ¿Hay algo en su habitación? _____
5. ¿Hay algo en su cartera (*wallet*)? _____
6. ¿Hay algo en su bolsillo (*pocket*)? _____

E. Answer these questions according to your house.

Example: **¿Hay alguien en la piscina?** → **Sí, hay alguien. No, no hay nadie.**

1. ¿Hay alguien en el jardín? _____
2. ¿Hay alguien en la casa? _____
3. ¿Hay alguien en el cuarto? _____
4. ¿Hay alguien en el baño? _____
5. ¿Hay alguien en la calle? _____
6. ¿Hay alguien en la cocina? _____

F. Answer these questions, first affirmatively, then, negatively.

Example: ¿Hay algunos cuadros (paintings) en el museo? → **Sí, hay algunos. No, no hay ninguno.** Remember: **Ningún, ninguno, and ninguna** do not have plural forms.

1. ¿Hay algunas flores en el jardín? _____
2. ¿Hay algunos niños en el colegio? _____
3. ¿Hay algunos libros en la biblioteca? _____
4. ¿Hay algunas personas en la fiesta? _____
5. ¿Hay algunas sillas en la clase? _____
6. ¿Hay algunos perros en el parque? _____

G. Express these sentences using double negatives.

Example: **Hay algo interesante en el cine** → **No hay nada interesante en el cine.**

1. Hay algo delicioso en la cocina: _____
2. Tengo algunas flores en mi jardín: _____
3. María también estudia allí: _____
4. Sofía siempre estudia la lección: _____
5. Meten algo en el coche: _____
6. Siempre reciben a sus amigos: _____
7. También venden bananas en esa verdulería: _____

H. Choose among these indefinite pronouns to complete the sentences: **nada - nadie - ningún - ninguna** or these negative adverbs: **nunca - ni - tampoco - jamás**

1. _____ hay _____ en el refrigerador.
2. María y Daniel _____ discuten.
3. No me gusta _____ la carne _____ el pollo.
4. No me gusta _____ aquel joven.
5. _____ sabe su nombre.
6. No quiero ir al restaurante. Él _____ quiere ir.
7. No hay _____ hotel en esta ciudad.
8. _____ flor es tan hermosa como esta.

I. Answer the following questions with a negative response. Try to use a double negative.

Remember: **Ningún, ninguno** and **ninguna do have plural forms but they exist in very specific cases.**

1. ¿Comparten ustedes algo?

   No,_____

2. ¿Tomás recibe algo por su cumpleaños (*for his birthday*)?

   No,_____

3. ¿Hay algún restaurante en esta (*this*) calle?

   No,_____

4. ¿Cantas a veces ?

   No,_____

5. ¿Ellos trabajaron algo por la mañana (*in the morning*)?

   No,_____

6. ¿Leen algún periódico los domingos?

   No,_____

7. ¿Hay alguna flor en el invierno?

   No,_____

8. ¿Siempre vas al supermercado los sábados?

   No,_____

9. ¿Los turistas visitan algún parque?

   No,_____

10. ¿Vosotros coméis algo de carne?

    No,_____

J. **Turn these sentences into negative ones. In some cases, it will be a double negative. Example: ¿Sabes algo de francés? <u>No, no sé nada de francés.</u>**

Remember: **Ningún, ninguno and ninguna have** plural forms, but they are seldom used.

1. Siempre está triste.

   _____

2. Nosotros hacemos algo de deporte hoy.

   _____

3. María necesita comprar libros también.

   _____

4. Este supermercado es algo pequeño.

   _____

5. Alguien estudia en la biblioteca.

   _____

6. Muchas niñas bailan en el colegio.

   _____

7. ¿Hay alguna verdulería aquí (here)?

   _____

8. Martín bebe agua.

   _____

9. Vosotros siempre limpiáis la casa.

   _____

10. Yo conozco a todos sus amigos.

    _____

Affirmative and negative sentences

CHAPTER 12:

CONJUNCTIONS AND INDEFINITE ADJECTIVES
YOU, AND YOU, AND YOU

12.1 Conjunctions

Don't be intimidated by that big word! Conjunctions are some of the most common components of everyday language. They connect other words, phrases, and clauses. For example, in that last sentence 'and' was the conjunction, because it unites the rest of the sentence.

Some other examples of conjunctions are 'or' and 'but.' They allow us to say things like 'She came by, but she didn't come in.'

By learning conjunctions in Spanish, you'll be able to construct slightly more complex sentences. Although they aren't hard to construct, they can convey a whole new layer of meaning.

In Spanish, there are two types of conjunctions:

- Coordinating conjunctions ('but,' 'and,' 'or')
- Subordinating conjunctions ('because,' 'although')

What's the difference?

Coordinating conjunctions join two parts of a sentence that are equal in importance, e.g., 'Tina loves Instagram *and* Bob loves Facebook.' You know they're equal because if you removed the conjunction, you would still understand that Tina loves Instagram and Bob loves Facebook.

Subordinating conjunctions, on the other hand, connect parts of a sentence that don't convey the same message when they're independent. E.g., 'Tina loves Instagram *because* she's a fan of photography.' If you removed the conjunction in this sentence, you wouldn't understand that the reason Tina loves Instagram is because she's a fan of photography.

These same differences apply to coordinating and subordinating conjunctions in Spanish. Understanding their purpose will help you navigate them.

Coordinating Conjunctions			
Combine Elements Together (Copulative Conjunctions)	y	and	Come **y** bebe (*he eats and drinks*).
	e	and (used when the word following the copulative conjunction "**y**" begins with "i" or the silent letter "h" followed by the vowel "i")	Andrés **e** Inés bailan en la fiesta (*Andres and Ines dance at the party*).
	ni	nor	No come **ni** pan **ni** galletitas (*He doesn't eat bread nor crackers*).
Show an Opposition or Difference (Adversative Conjunctions)	pero	but	Es inteligente **pero** perezoso (*He's intelligent but lazy*).
	mas	but	Tiene un trabajo **mas** no es feliz (*She has a job but isn't happy*).
	sin embargo (usually used after a semi-colon)	however, nevertheless, but	Tiene mucho dinero; **sin embargo**, no lo comparte (*She has a lot of money but doesn't share it*).
	aunque	even if, though, although	La película es buena, **aunque** larga (*The movie is good, even if it's long*).
	sino	but	No come carne **sino** pescado.

Coordinating Conjunctions

Show Options (Disjunctive Conjunctions)	**o**	*or*	María regresa a las 12:00 p.m. **o** a la 1:00 p.m. (*María comes back at 12:00 p.m. or at 1:00 p.m.*).
	u	*or (used when the word following the disjunctive conjunction "o" begins with the vowel "o" or the silent letter "h" followed by the vowel "o")*	Laura organiza **u** ordena los papeles (*Laura organizes or arranges the papers*).
Show Alternation (Distributive Conjunctions)	**o... o**	*either... or*	**O** estudias **o** no miras televisión (*either you study, or you don't watch TV*).
	bien... bien	*either... or*	**Bien** estudian en el parque, **bien** en la biblioteca (*either they study in the park or in the library*).
Show Alternation (Distributive Conjunctions)	**tanto... como**	*both*	**Tanto** Pedro **como** María son buenos estudiantes (*both Pedro and María are good students*).
	ya... ya	*whether... or*	El matrimonio es compartir la vida **ya** en las alegrías, **ya** en las tristezas (*Marriage is sharing life whether in happiness or in sorrow*).

> **Tip:** The conjunction **y** is replaced by **e** before words starting with **i** or **hi** for reasons of pronunciation. Example: **Tomates e higos** (*tomatoes and figs*).
>
> For the same reason, **o** is replaced with **u** before words starting with **o** or **ho**. Example: **Apartamentos u hoteles**.

Theory, step aside; it's practice time!

12.1. Practice

A. **Find the right conjunctions: y - e - o - u. If the sentence is not translated, go ahead, and translate it.**

1. María and Inés: _____

2. There are ten or eleven children: _____

3. Get the key and try to open the door: Toma la llave _____ intenta abrir la puerta.

4. He calls and invites us: _____

5. She saw something or heard a noise: Vio algo _____ oyó un ruido.

6. She knows how to read and write very well. _____

B. **Fill in the blanks with the conjunctions y, o, or pero**

1. El niño come una banana _____ una manzana.

2. ¿Martín trabaja _____ estudia?

3. Busco a mi perro _____ no lo encuentro.

4. Lo repito dos _____ tres veces (*times*).

5. Cantasteis _____ bailasteis toda la noche.

6. Soy francés _____ vivo en Italia.

7. Llegas a las ocho _____ nueve de la mañana.

8. Luisa trabaja mucho _____ gana (*earns*) poco (little).

C. **Let's practice adversative conjunctions: pero, más, sin embargo, aunque, sino. Fill in the blanks with the right conjunction:**

1. Como poco _____ estoy gordo.

2. No trabaja hoy en la oficina _____ mañana

3. Tomás sabe mucho _____ es una persona humilde (*humble*).

4. Tiene coche; _____ le gusta caminar.

5. Viaja mucho, _____ no tiene mucho dinero.

6. _____ yo no recibo el periódico, lo leo todos los días.

D. **Circle the right conjunction in each sentence.**

1. Camino todos los días { porque - sin embargo } es bueno para la salud.

2. Ellos comen en un restaurante todos los días { pero - ni } ellas comen en casa.

3. Teresa aprende alemán { ni - aunque } no lo necesita.

4. { Aunque - Ni } Elena { aunque - ni } Cristián beben vino.

5. Elena { y - e } Hilario son abogados.

6. { Aunque - Tanto } Pedro { como - ni } Sofía son franceses.

7. Compramos { y - pero } vendemos ropa usada (*used clothes*).

8. Estudia mucho; { aunque - sin embargo } no aprende mucho.

Conjunctions and indefinite adjectives

12.2 Subordinating Conjunctions

As we mentioned earlier, subordinating conjunctions connect parts of a sentence that are dependent on each other.

Subordinating Conjunctions			
Showing Cause (Cause Conjunctions)	**porque**	because	Ella está cansada **porque** trabaja mucho (*She's tired because she works a lot*).
	pues	since, as, because	Estoy en casa **pues** llueve (*I'm home because it's raining*).
	como	since, as, because	**Como** está ocupado, no tiene tiempo (*Since he's busy, he doesn't have any time*).
Elaborating (Relative Conjunctions)	**que**	that	Me dijo **que** soy su mejor amigo (*He told me that I was his best friend*).
Making Comparisons (Comparative Conjunctions)	**así como**	just as	José es alto, **así como** su hermana (*José is tall, just as his sister*).
	así también	so to	Sabe francés, **así también** alemán (*He knows French, so too German*).
	tal como	as	María es simpática **tal como** Clara (*Maria is as nice as Clara*).
To Show an Obstacle Doesn't Prevent Action (Concessive Conjunctions)	**aunque**	although, even though, though	La biblioteca está cerrada, **aunque** son las 12:00 p.m. (*The library is closed, even though it's 12:00 p.m.*).
	a pesar de que	even though, despite the fact that	Está triste, **a pesar de que** tiene muchos amigos (*He's sad, despite the fact that he has lots of friends*).
To Show Conditions (Conditional Conjunctions)	**si**	if	Pago con tarjeta **si** lo necesito (*I pay with a credit card if I need to*).
	a menos que	unless	Corro todos los días **a menos que** llueva (*I run every day unless it rains*).

Subordinating Conjunctions			
To Give a Sense of Time and Order (Time Conjunctions)	mientras	while, meanwhile	Camina **mientras** habla por teléfono (*She walks while she talks on the phone*).

Common Mistakes: The conjunction **que** is essential in Spanish, even though it is often not translated in English. **Que** as a conjunction which means *that*.

Creo que ella es feliz (*I believe that she is happy*)

Note that in English, you can say, *I believe she is happy* (without the "that"). Be careful! You can't say **Creo es feliz** in Spanish, omitting the **que**. You absolutely need the **que**.

Creo la niña es feliz X
Creo que la niña es feliz ✓

Ready to flex those newfound skills? It's practice time!

12.2. Practice

A. Let's practice the relative conjunction si. Join these sentences and conjugate the verbs. Example: **María / no/ saber/ si / Juan / necesitar / algo: María no sabe si Juan necesita algo.**

1. Pedro y Luis / no / saber / si / sus amigos / regresar / hoy:
   _____

2. Mirta / pregunta (*ask*) / si / hay / examen / mañana:
   _____

3. José / decidir / si / subir / el monte Fitz Roy:
   _____

4. Vosotros / no / saber / si / Paula / necesitar / algo / para la fiesta:
   _____

5. Usted / preguntar / si / los empleados / trabajar / bien:
   _____

6. Tú / decidir / si / beber / café / o / té:
   _____

Speak Abroad
Academy

B. Let's practice the relative conjunction que. Remember? The one you should never omit in Spanish. Join these sentences.

Example: Tenemos una fiesta. Me dice. → **Me dice que tenemos una fiesta.**

1. Vivimos en la calle Oro. Ella sabe: _____
2. Viajamos todo el año. Juan piensa: _____
3. El señor Ortiz arregla hornos. Yo creo: _____
4. A José le gusta comer. Juana dice: _____
5. Es tarde. La profesora nos dice: _____
6. Los niños necesitan lápices nuevos. La madre dice:
_____

C. Join both sentences with a subordinate conjunction: porque - pero - aunque - que.
Example: Es un buen profesor. Yo creo → **Yo creo que es un buen profesor.**

1. Me gusta. Mis hijos ordenan solos.
2. Trabajo mucho. Gano poco.
3. Hace frío. Hay sol.
4. Martín cree. Está demasiado ventoso para correr.
5. El verdulero me explica. Los tomates están verdes.
6. Llegas temprano. Sales temprano.

12.3 Indefinite Adjectives

An indefinite adjective is an adjective used to describe a noun in a non-specific way. It agrees with the noun in number and sometimes gender. Many indefinite adjectives in Spanish are identical to Spanish indefinite pronouns.

Examples of indefinite adjectives are:

Hay **pocas** manzanas (*There are a few apples*).

Tiene **alguna** posibilidad (*possibility*) de viajar (*travel*).

Hay **mucho** sol.

Es la **misma** casa.

Necesito **algún** vestido.

El profesor explica **todos** los ejercicios.

SINGULAR		PLURAL		
masculine	feminine	masculine	feminine	
algún	alguna	algunos	algunas	*some, a few*
ningún	ninguna	-	-	*none, neither*
cada	cada	-	-	*each*
cierto	cierta	ciertos	ciertas	*certain*
mismo	misma	mismos	mismas	*same*
mucho	mucha	muchos	muchas	*many, much, a lot*
otro	otra	otros	otras	*other*
poco	poca	pocos	pocas	*few, a little*
tal	-	tales	-	*some, any*
tanto	tanta	tantos	tantas	*so many, so much*
todo	toda	todos	todas	*all*
-	-	varios	varias	*several, some*

Common Mistake:

Indefinite adjectives are used in place of an article, **not with one**.

X Don't say: **Hay las algunas manzanas**

✓ Say instead: **Hay algunas manzanas**

Rules, step aside; it's practice time!

12.3. Practice

A. Complete the sentences with the right indefinite adjective.

Example: **Pablo solo compra** _____ **manzanas** → **Pablo solo compra unas manzanas.**

1. _____ personas trabajan en su casa.
2. Hay _____ pájaros que parece (*looks like*) una selva (*jungle*)
3. Es el _____ sombrero que tiene Juan.
4. Susana tiene _____ casa en la playa.
5. _____ personas comparten apartamento con amigos.
6. _____ día que pasa es peor (*is worse*).
7. Ese cantante compuso (*composed*) _____ canciones parecidas (*similar*).
8. Llueve_____ la semana.

B. Translate the following sentences with conjunctions and indefinite adjectives:

1. Ella tiene muchos perros y gatos.

   _____

2. María tiene varias hijas, pero no tiene hijos.

   _____

3. Tanto Luis como Juan tienen pocos amigos.

   _____

4. No lee ni revistas (*magazines*) ni periódicos (*newspapers*).

   _____

5. Conoce otros países pues viaja mucho.

   _____

6. Tiene el mismo coche que Laura.

   _____

7. Conoce cada calle de París, pero no conoce su propia ciudad (*her own city*).

   _____

8. Habla algunos idiomas, pero no habla inglés.

   _____

9. Es la misma amistad, aunque somos más viejos.

   _____

10. Todos los idiomas son útiles (*useful*), aunque algunos son más útiles (*useful*) que otros.

    _____

C. Elena has a positive outlook on life. Roberto has a negative outlook on life. Change Elena's statements to the opposite to know what Robert thinks.

Example: **Tengo pocos problemas → Tengo muchos problemas.**

1. Todos los días son hermosos → _____
2. Tengo pocas tristezas → _____
3. Hay tantas cosas lindas en la vida → _____
4. Tengo muchos amigos → _____
5. Ciertos días son malos → _____
6. Ninguna tarea (*task*) es imposible → _____

CHAPTER 13:

LIKES AND DISLIKES

I LIKE APPLES

It would be impossible to get to know other people and allow them to get to know you without learning to express likes and dislikes. They convey our opinions and other key parts of our personality. By using **me gusta** and **no me gusta**, we can finally tell people what we really think!

13.1 Constructions With Me Gusta and No Me Gusta

> **Poema XV**
>
> **Pablo Neruda**
>
> Me gusta cuando callas
> Porque estás como ausente,
> Y me oyes desde lejos,
> Y mi voz no te toca. [...]

"I like it when you're silent / because you're sort of absent / and you hear me from afar / and my voice doesn't touch you."

This is part of a poem by Chilean poet Pablo Neruda (1904-1973), who wrote in various styles, including passionate love poems, and won the Nobel Prize in Literature in 1971.

The verb **gustar** is used in Spanish to express likes and dislikes:

⮑ **Me gusta leer** (*I like to read*)

⮑ **No me gustan los gatos** (*I don't like cats*)

But **gustar** does not literally mean *to like*.

Strictly speaking, *gustar* means *to be pleasing (to someone)*. It needs to be used with an indirect object to make complete sense. This indirect object is whatever it is you're expressing your affection or fondness for.

The indirect object can be a pronoun (me, te, le, nos, os, le) or a person/object/animal preceded by a → a + person/name/object.

For example:

A María le gusta el helado (*Maria likes ice-cream*)

A mí me gustan los caballos (*I like horses*)

A Juan y Cristina les gusta la música clásica (*Juan and Cristina like classical music*).

A sentence like, **A Martín le gusta la comida** has two indirect objects: **le** and **a Martin. A Martín** is used to add emphasis or to clarify who or what the indirect object pronoun is (**le** could be a woman, an animal, or almost anything).

Notice, too, that the verb **gustar** must agree with its subject, i.e., the person or thing that is liked, *not* the person who is being described. In the sentences above, we used both **gusta** and **gustan** to agree with the different nouns.

A Martín le gustan los caballos → gustan matches **caballos**, not Martín.

To say that you *don't* like something, you need to add **no** before the indirect object pronoun.

No me gustan los perros (*I don't like dogs*)

No les gustan los gatos (*they don't like cats*)

No nos gustan las motos (*we don't like motorcycles*)

Indirect Object Pronouns

me: for me

te: for you

le: for you, him, her, it

nos: for us

os: for you

les: for you, them

Now check these sentences:

- **A Martín le gustan los mapas**: *Martin likes maps (or Maps are pleasing to Martin)*. In this case, since maps is plural, "gustan" is in the plural form. **Le** is the indirect object and **A Martin** is used in addition to the indirect object pronoun for clarification or emphasis.

- **A mí me gusta el deporte**: *I like sports (or Sports are pleasing to me)*. Again, **deporte** agrees with the singular **gusta**. **Me** is the indirect object pronoun and **A mí** is used as emphasis.

↻ **¿A usted le gustan las flores?:** *Do you like flowers?* (*Are flowers pleasing to you?*). **Las flores** agrees with the plural **gustan**. **Le** is the indirect object. **A usted** is used for clarification (since **le** can also refer to someone else).

↻ **A ellos les gusta el teatro**: *They like the theatre* (*The theatre is pleasing to them*). **El teatro** is singular and agrees with **gusta**. The indirect object is **les** and **A ellos** is used for emphasis.

Tip: Just as in English, you can combine **like + a verb** (*I like running*). In Spanish, **gustar** is combined with the **infinitive** of the verb (not the gerund, like in English): **gustar + verbo en infinitivo**.

Example: **Te gusta correr** (*you like running*), **me gusta ver televisión** (*I like watching TV*), **les gusta cocinar** (*they like cooking*).

X Do not say: Me gusta corriendo
✓ Say: Me gusta correr

Vocabulary: Food

Something that we all have strong opinions about is food! It's time to expand your vocabulary and get to know the different Spanish words for food. Using what we just learned, can you express which types of food below you like or dislike?

English	Spanish	Pronunciation
meat	**carne**	*[kahr-neh]*
chicken	**pollo**	*[poh-yoh]*
fish	**pescado**	*[pehs-kah-doh]*
hamburgers	**hamburguesas**	*[ahm-boor-geh-sahs]*
tomato	**tomate**	*[toh-mah-teh]*
lettuce	**lechuga**	*[leh-choo-gah]*
apple	**manzana**	*[mahn-thah-nah]*
orange	**naranja**	*[nah-rahng-hah]*
potatoes	**papa**	*[pah-pah]*
banana	**banana**	*[bah-nah-nah]*
onion	**cebolla**	*[theh-boh-yah]*
bread	**pan**	*[pahn]*
milk	**leche**	*[leh-cheh]*
water	**agua**	*[ah-gwah]*
coffee	**café**	*[kah-feh]*

English	Spanish	Pronunciation
tea	**té**	*[teh]*
sugar	**azúcar**	*[ah-thoo-khar]*
candy	**caramelos**	*[kah-rah-meh-lohs]*

Enough scribbling on the language map; let's navigate through the terrain of practice!

13.1. Practice

A. Write an indirect object pronoun for each subject pronoun.

1. A nosotros _____ gusta.
2. A vosotros _____ gusta.
3. A ustedes _____ gusta.
4. A ellos _____ gusta.
5. A Juan y Matías _____ gusta.
6. A mí _____ gusta.
7. A ti _____ gusta.
8. A Juan _____ gusta.
9. A Elena _____ gusta.

B. Translate the following with the two indirect objects.

Example: **She likes candy → <u>A ella le gustan los caramelos.</u>**

1. I like the car _____
2. They like onions _____
3. We don't like reading _____
4. You (sing.) like bananas _____
5. You (inf.pl.) like working _____
6. Marcos likes studying _____
7. Elsa likes tomatoes _____
8. My father likes to eat _____
9. My mother likes fish _____
10. The boys don't like milk _____
11. Maria likes chicken _____

C. Join the words to make a sentence. Make sure you include two indirect objects (the pronoun + whoever the action is for). Example: **no / las / gustan /le / bananas / a Mirta: <u>A Mirta no le gustan las bananas</u>**.

1. nos / correr / a nosotros / gusta:

    _____

2. no / gustan / las verduras / les / a los niños

    _____

3. esos zapatos / gustan / a mí / me

    _____

4. las fiestas / a Luis y Teresa / gustan / les

    _____

5. tocar piano / a Elena / gusta / le

    _____

6. gusta / me / a mí / el pescado

    _____

D. Pick one of the items below and say you like it. Pick the other one to say you don't like it. You can switch the items according to what you like. You may use an adversative conjunction (**pero, aunque, sin embargo**) or a copulative conjunction (**y**).

Example: **¿comer carne? ¿comer pescado?** <u>No me gusta comer carne, pero me gusta comer pescado.</u>

1. ¿Leo Messi? ¿Cristiano Ronaldo?

    _____

2. ¿comer hamburguesas? ¿comer pastas?

    _____

3. ¿el café? ¿el té?

    _____

4. ¿la actriz Meryl Streep? ¿la actriz Judy Dench?

    _____

5. ¿el tenista Medvedev? ¿el tenista Federer?

    _____

6. ¿estudiar en la biblioteca? ¿estudiar en el comedor?

    _____

7. ¿los perros? ¿los gatos?

    _____

8. ¿viajar en tren? ¿viajar en coche?

    _____

E. Complete the sentences by conjugating **gustar** according to its subject and adding the right pronoun (le/les). Example: **A Isabel** _____**los niños** → **A Isabel le gustan los niños.**

1. A Sebastián y Nicolás _____ los deportes.

2. A vosotros _____ los relojes caros.

3. A ti _____ las motos.

4. A nosotros _____ aprender español.

5. A mí _____ los chocolates.

6. A usted _____ los coches.

F. Complete these questions making **gustar** concur with the subject and adding the appropriate personal pronoun. Example: **(él / gustar)** _____ el teatro? → **¿A él le gusta el teatro?**

1. ¿(nosotros / gustar) _____ las fiestas?

2. ¿(Teresa / gustar)_____ su universidad?

3. ¿(ellos / gustar) _____ recibir gente en su casa?

4. ¿(yo / gustar) _____ hacer yoga?

5. ¿(Tú / gustar) _____ el pescado?

6. ¿(usted / gustar) _____ viajar?

G. Complete with a + pronoun + pronoun + verb **gustar**.

Example **(yo) estudiar idiomas→ A mí me gusta estudiar idiomas.**

1. _____ (nosotros) trabajar.

2. _____ (ustedes) vivir solos.

3. _____ (vosotros) caminar en el parque los sábados.

4. _____ (Carolina y Luis) subir montañas.

5. _____ (tú) invitar amigos a tu casa.

6. _____ (ellos) viajar por el mundo.

H. Rewrite these sentences by correcting the mistakes on the Indirect Object Pronouns:

1. A mí nos gustan los caramelos: _____

2. A ti le gusta el pan: _____

3. A vosotros me gusta la leche: _____

4. A ti me gusta el café _____

5. A ellos nos gustan las naranjas: _____

6. A él te gusta la carne: _____

Vocabulary: Members of the Family

English	Spanish	Pronunciation
father	**padre**	*[pah-dreh]*
mother	**madre**	*[mah-dreh]*
daughter	**hija**	*[ee-hah]*
son	**hijo**	*[ee-hoh]*
grandfather	**abuelo**	*[ah-bweh-loh]*
grandmother	**abuela**	*[ah-bweh-lah]*
uncle/aunt	**tío/tía**	*[tee-oh/tee-ah]*
cousin	**primo/a**	*[pree-moh/pree-mah]*
nephew/niece	**sobrino/a**	*[soh-bree-noh/soh-bree-nah]*

I.   **¿Adónde vamos en las vacaciones (***Where do we go on vacations?***)**

The Pérez family each have their own idea of a good vacation and where they prefer to go. Turn the suggested separate elements into a sentence. Remember to include the indirect object that clarifies or adds emphasis.

Example: ⟶ **padre / nadar Al padre le gusta nadar.**

1.   abuelo / cocinar

   _____

2.   hermano / hacer surf (*to do surf*)

   _____

3.   tía / leer libros

   _____

4.   primos / comprar ropa (*go shopping for clothes*)

   _____

5.   padre / comer y beber

   _____

6.   hija / buscar caracoles en la orilla (*look for seashells on the shore*)

   _____

7.   madre / la tranquilidad

   _____

8.   sobrinos / correr por la playa (*run on the beach*)

   _____

13.2 Expressing Wants in a Direct and Polite Way

You've learned how to express your likes and dislikes, but what about your wants? How can you tell someone that you want something?"

In Spanish, you use the verb **querer** to express **wants**, e.g., **Yo quiero un café** (*I want a coffee*)

How do you say you don't want something? For this, we'll use **no** again.

To say you don't want something, just add a **no** before the verb: **Yo no quiero un café** (*I don't want a coffee*)

As with **gustar,** you can also add an infinitive to **querer** when you *want to do something*, e.g., **Quiero aprender alemán** (*I want to learn German*).

Sometimes it's not polite to ask directly for something. For example, if you're asking for a map in a hotel lobby, it's more polite to say, **Me gustaría un mapa (***I would like a map) than **Quiero un mapa** (*I want a map*).

When you want to express what you would like or wouldn't like, in Spanish you say, **Me gustaría / No me gustaría**.

Of course, **gustaría** is also used when you're wishing or pining for something: **Me gustaría conocer a Luis** (*I would like to meet Luis*). In other words, it's a way of expressing your wants in a less direct way, which is essential for politeness.

With **gustaría** you can also add an infinitive for something you *would like to do*: **Me gustaría subir el Everest**.

13.2. Practice

Choose what you would say in each scenario, depending on whether you can be more direct or need to be more polite:

1. You're at a bar and ask the waiter for a glass of water:
    { Quiero | me gustaría } un vaso de agua.
2. You're expressing your need for sleep to a friend:
    { Quiero | me gustaría } dormir.
3. You're explaining to a professor that you would like to speak Spanish well:
    { Me gustaría | quiero } hablar bien español.
4. You're asking a salesperson at a store to hand you that green dress:
    { Quiero | me gustaría } ese vestido verde.
5. You're telling your friend you want to fix the roof:
    { Quiero | me gustaría } arreglar el techo.

CHAPTER 14:

PREPOSITIONS I
THE HAT IS ON THE CHAIR

14.1 Introduction to Prepositions

Again, don't be afraid of the big word. We use prepositions all the time and they're not complex. They're words like 'on,' 'over,' or 'until,' which are important for describing space and time.

If you're trying to help someone find something, prepositions allow you to describe to them which part of the room they would find the object in. Is it *under* the bed? *On* the table? *In* the laundry hamper?

It also describes time. If you're trying to organize plans with your friends, prepositions would help you arrange an appropriate time. Can you only hang out *at* 8 PM? *After* work? *Before* your favorite TV show starts playing? Or maybe just *until* you start feeling drunk?

The good news is that, unlike most words in Spanish, prepositions in Spanish don't change! They have no number or gender, and always remain the same. Phew!

Here is the list of simple prepositions:

English	Spanish	Pronunciation
at, to	**a**	*[ah]*
before	**ante**	*[ahn-teh]*
under	**bajo**	*[bah-hoh]*
with	**con**	*[kohn]*
against	**contra**	*[kohn-trah]*
of, from	**de**	*[deh]*
after, since, from	**desde**	*[dehs-deh]*
during	**durante**	*[doo-rahn-teh]*
in, on	**en**	*[ehn]*
among, between	**entre**	*[ehn-treh]*
toward	**hacia**	*[ah-thyah]*
until, up to, as far as	**hasta**	*[ahs-tah]*
except	**menos**	*[meh-nohs]*

Speak Abroad
Academy

English	Spanish	Pronunciation
for, in order to	**para**	*[pah-rah]*
by, for	**por**	*[pohr]*
except, save	**salvo**	*[sahl-boh]*
according to	**según**	*[seh-goon]*
without	**sin**	*[seen]*
on, upon, over, above	**sobre**	*[soh-breh]*
after, behind	**tras**	*[trahs]*

Most Common Prepositions: en - de - con

Let's start practicing the three most common prepositions in Spanish. We will start with these three:

en	*in, on*	States the idea of remaining in a place or time	Juan está **en** su cama *(Juan is in his bed).*
de	*of, from*	Gives the idea of possession, matter, or origin	La casa es **de** Gabriela *(The house belongs to Gabriela).* La silla es **de** madera *(The chair is made of wood).*
con	*with*	Indicates company	Estoy **con** mis amigos *(I'm with my friends).*

Time to roll up your sleeves and practice!

14.1. Practice

A. Complete the following sentences with the prepositions en, de, or con:

1. Luis vive _____ una ciudad grande.
2. María viaja siempre _____ su hermana.
3. La casa es _____ color amarillo.
4. Los zapatos son _____ cuero (*leather*).
5. Ustedes están _____ el jefe.
6. Hay parques hermosos _____ París.
7. El gato es _____ Pedro.
8. Mi sobrina trabaja _____ su padre.
9. Estoy _____ Inglaterra.

B. Again, try to complete these sentences with **en, de, or con**

1. Flavia cumple el cuatro _____ abril _____ 2000.
2. Me gustaría un café _____ leche.
3. Esta cartera es _____ Simón.
4. Regresa de la oficina _____ bicicleta.
5. Tengo una buena relación _____ mis padres (*my parents*).
6. Tengo una casa _____ ocho ventanas.

C. Try completing the sentences by choosing between **en and entre**

1. Mis abuelos manejan (*drive*) _____ coche por la ciudad.
2. Tomás está _____ su casa.
3. Felipe está sentado (*sitting*) _____ María y Pablo.
4. El señor Pérez regresa a su casa _____ las ocho y las nueve de la noche.
5. Le regalamos un perro a Sebastián _____ los amigos (*among the friends*).
6. Las flores florecen (*bloom*) _____ primavera.

14.2 Other Common Prepositions: a - para - sin

a	to	Indicates movement towards a goal, whether real or imagined. It is used before an indirect object and a direct object when it's a person.	Camino **a** mi casa (*I walk to my house*). Busco **a** mi hermana *but* busco los perros.
para	*for, in order to*	Indicates the aim or purpose of an action	El lápiz es **para** mi hija (*The pencil is for my daughter*).
sin	*without*	Indicates lack of	El hotel **sin** turistas (*The hotel is without tourists*).

What follows a preposition?

⮩ In Spanish, prepositions can be followed by verbs in the infinitive form (the verbs that usually end in **-r!**): **Tomás estudia para aprender** (*Tomas studies to learn*) or **Martín habla sin pensar** (*Martin speaks without thinking*).

⮩ Prepositions can be followed by nouns: **María compra una flor para su madre** (*María buys a flower for her mother*).

⮩ Prepositions can be followed by pronouns: **El libro es para ella** (*The book is for her*). In Spanish, the pronouns that follow prepositions are **subject pronouns**, except for **mí** and **ti** (instead of **yo** and **tú**): **El café es para mí** and **El té es para ti**.

Speak Abroad
Academy

> **Tip:** When you use the preposition **con** together with the **1ˢᵗ and 2ⁿᵈ subject pronoun**, the result is **conmigo** and **contigo**. In fact, **con** is the only preposition that combines with a pronoun. Example: **Mi esposo siempre viaja conmigo** (*My husband always travels with me*) or **Hablo en el parque contigo** (*I talk with you in the park*).

Eager to dance with phrases? Let's groove through practice!

14.2. Practice

A. Complete the following sentences with the prepositions **a, para,** or **sin.**

1. El regalo es _____ Juan.
2. Me gusta el café _____ azúcar.
3. El padre regresa _____ su casa a las 9:00 p.m.
4. Ella estudia _____ aprender.
5. Mi mamá corre _____ la sala.
6. Elena aprende alemán _____ profesores.
7. Mi tío entra _____ la oficina a las 8:00 p.m.
8. Tomás viaja _____ mapas.

B. Complete the following sentences adding a just when it's needed:

1. José le pregunta _____ María cuándo regresa su mamá.
2. Por favor, describe _____ un león.
3. Teresa busca _____ los perros para darles de comer.
4. Silvia patea _____ la puerta.
5. En el océano hay _____ peces.
6. Busca _____ su mamá.

C. Complete the following sentences choosing **a** or **de.**

1. Los estudiantes regresan _____ su casa _____ las ocho de la noche.
2. El martes voy _____ Madrid.
3. Pedro hace ejercicio _____ noche, no _____ día.
4. Son las cinco _____ la tarde.
5. Sofía es _____ Chile.
6. Su padre le regala _____ su hija un perro.
7. Luis viene _____ hablar con el doctor.
8. Esa botella es _____ plástico.

D. Complete these sentences choosing between **desde** and **de.**

1. Regresa _____ la fiesta a las cuatro de la mañana.
2. Camina _____ su casa hasta el trabajo.
3. Me gustan los platos _____ madera.
4. Miramos a la gente _____ el balcón.

5. Estudia en ese colegio _____ los tres años.
6. Vende vestidos _____ su casa.

14.3 Other Common Prepositions: hasta - por - según - para - contra

hasta	until, up to, as far as	Expresses a limit	Camina **hasta** la cocina (*He/she walks up to the kitchen*).
por	by, for	Describes the means or cause for something. Also precedes a quantity of time.	Viaja **por** barco (*He/she travels by boat*). Camina **por** dos horas (*She walks for two hours*).
según	according to	Used to describe the opinion of others. It's used before names and pronouns.	**Según** mi mamá, la película es mala (*According to my mom, the film is bad*).
para	for, in order to	Used for deadlines, and to indicate purpose and destination	El regalo es **para** mi amiga (*The present is for my friend*)
contra	against	Describes opposition	La lucha **contra** el cambio climático (*The battle against climate change*)

Excited to play with sentences? Let's do it!

14.3.   Practice

A. See if you can complete these sentences with the right preposition from this last group: hasta - para - por - según - contra

1. El hombre salta _____ la ventana.
2. El regalo es _____ su hijo.
3. _____ mi amiga, el restaurante es malo.
4. Caminamos _____ el parque.
5. Ella mira televisión _____ una hora.
6. Estoy _____ las ideas de ese profesor.
7. Está en mi casa _____ el martes.
8. Hay una habitación _____ dos personas.
9. _____ el doctor, debes comer muchas verduras y frutas.

Speak Abroad
Academy

B. Complete the sentences with the right preposition from this list:

hasta - para - según - contra

1. Este océano (*ocean*) llega _____ las costas africanas (*the African coasts*).
2. _____ mi hermano, hoy los bancos están cerrados.
3. El Día de la Madre, compro un regalo _____ mi mamá.
4. En la carrera (*race*), nadaron _____ la corriente (*against the current*)
5. Nuestro padre no regresa a casa _____ las nueve de la noche.
6. El barco navega (*sails*) _____ Londres.

C. And now that you're more familiar with these prepositions, try to tackle the whole list with these sentences, filling in the blanks. These are the prepositions that you need:

a - entre - sobre - sin - con - para - según - hacia - por - sobre - durante

1. No corro _____ zapatillas deportivas.
2. María lleva su cartera _____ ella.
3. Estos regalos son _____ mis amigos.
4. _____ Pablo, la película es buena.
5. Los niños corren _____ nosotros.
6. El profesor habla _____ física cuántica (quantum physics).
7. Luis corre _____ dos horas
8. El libro está _____ la mesa.
9. El coche está _____ los dos árboles.
10. Busco _____ a mi padre.

CHAPTER 15:

PREPOSITIONS II

THE BOX IS BEHIND THE CHAIR

Did you think we were done with prepositions? There are so many of them, and they're all so important. Let's look at some more of them. These, in particular, are crucial for describing where something is located.

15.1 Prepositions for Talking About Place and Position

Compound prepositions are prepositions that are used to describe a **location** or **position**.

al lado de	*next to*
alrededor de	*around*
cerca de	*near*
debajo de	*underneath*
bajo	*under (more figurative than debajo de)*
delante de	*before, in front of (physical location)*
ante	*before, in front of, in the presence of*
dentro de	*inside of*
detrás de	*behind*
tras	*after (in a set of expressions)*
encima de	*on top of*
enfrente de, frente a	*in front of, opposite, facing, across from*
fuera de	*outside of*
junto a, pegado a	*close to, right next to*
lejos de	*far from*

Speak Abroad
Academy

Vocabulary: Objects in a Home

A great way to practice these new prepositions you've learned is by using them with common household objects. How is your home arranged? Can you describe it using the prepositions you just learned?

English	Spanish	Pronunciation
bookcase	librero	[bee-blyoh-teh-kah]
desk	escritorio	[ehs-kree-toh-ryoh]
chair	silla	[see-yah]
computer	computadora	[kohm-poo-tah-doh-rah]
backpack	mochila	[moh-chee-lah]
picture	cuadro	[kwah-droh]
clock	reloj	[rreh-lohh]
shelf	estante	[ehs-tahn-teh]
toys	juguetes	[hoo-geh-tes]
ball	pelota	[peh-loh-tah]
stuffed teddy bear	oso de peluche	[oh-soh deh peh-loo-cheh]
car	coche	[koh-cheh]
helicopter	helicóptero	[eh-lee-kohp-teh-roh]
pencil/pencils	lápiz/lápices	[lah-peeth/lah-pee-thes]
pencil holder	portalápices	[pohr-tah lah-pee-thes]
plant	planta	[plahn-tah]
box	caja	[kah-hah]
rug	alfombra	[ahl-fohm-brah]

Tip: In Spanish de + el contract to form **del: La calle del correo** (*the street of the post office/ the post office street*) and a + el contract to form **al: Camina al comedor (***she walks up to the dining room***).**

Tip: Notice that when **al lado de** precedes **el**, it becomes **al lado del.** The same happens with other prepositions.

Ready to apply what you know? Let's practice!

15.1. Practice

A. **Fill in the blanks with the correct compound preposition:**

1. La pelota está _____ (inside of) la caja.
2. La pelota está _____ (outside of) la caja.
3. La pelota está _____ (on top of) la caja.
4. La pelota está _____ (underneath) la caja.
5. La pelota está _____ (right next to) la caja.
6. La pelota está _____ (far from) la caja.

B. **Give the opposites of these compound prepositions:**

1. Dentro de → _____
2. Detrás de → _____
3. Cerca de → _____
4. Encima de → _____
5. Al lado de → _____

C. **Fill in the blanks with the correct compound preposition. Remember, that if the compound preposition has a de and is followed by the article el, you should contract both. Example: La niña está __debajo del__ (debajo + de + el) árbol**

1. El coche está _____ (behind) camión.
2. La cartera está _____ (inside of) la bolsa.
3. La silla está _____ (in front of) la mesa.
4. La mochila está _____ (on top of) la cama.
5. El gato está _____ (outside of) la casa.
6. El perro descansa (*rests*) _____ (under) el puente (*bridge*).

D. **In this neighborhood, there is a main square surrounded by a church, the post office and the town hall, one next to the other. Behind the post office is the movie theater. There is a clock on top of the town hall. In the middle of the square there is a large park. On one of the sides of the square, there is a bar. The supermarket is twenty blocks away.**

Choose a word from the first, second, and third column to form sentences. You're also going to need a verb. "Estar" is probably the verb to use. Though you may also use "Hay". Example: **La iglesia está delante de la plaza.**

la iglesia	lejos de	el bar
el correo	cerca de	la iglesia
el edificio municipal	detrás de	el cine

Speak Abroad
Academy

el bar	debajo de	el correo
el cine	junto a	el edificio municipal
la plaza	delante de	la plaza
el supermercado	encima de	reloj

1. _____

2. _____

3. _____

4. _____

5. _____

E. Translate the following sentences describing where the objects in a room are located by using the right preposition.

Example: The ball is next to the desk. **La pelota está** _____ **el escritorio.** = **La pelota está al lado del escritorio.**

1. The chair is in front of the desk: La silla está _____ el escritorio.
2. The computer is on top of the desk: La computadora está _____ el escritorio.
3. The plant is underneath the picture: La planta está _____ el cuadro.
4. The toys are inside the box: Los juguetes están _____ la caja.
5. The stuffed teddy bear is in front of the box: El oso de peluche está _____ la caja.
6. The red car is right next to the stuffed teddy bear: El coche rojo está _____ el oso de peluche.

F. Translate the following sentences describing where the objects in a room are located by using the right preposition.

1. The backpack is far from the bookcase: La mochila está _____ del librero.
2. The painting is near the bookcase: El cuadro está _____ la biblioteca.
3. The pencils are inside the pencil holder: Los lápices están _____ el portalápices.
4. The stuffed teddy bear is outside the box: El oso peluche está _____ la caja.
5. The map is on the wall: El mapa está _____ la pared.
6. The ball is under the desk: La pelota está _____ del escritorio.

15.2 Expressing origin

In Spanish you use the preposition, **de,** to express where you're from: **Yo soy de Perú** or **ustedes son de Bélgica.**

And to ask where you're from, you need to use the preposition **de + ** adverb **donde,** as in **¿De dónde eres tú?** (*Where are you from?*).

Time to roll up your sleeves and practice!

15.2. Practice

A. Answer these questions according to the clues. Remember that you don't need to use the subject pronoun, as it is already implied in the verb form.

Example: **¿De dónde eres tú? (Francia).** <u>Soy de Francia.</u>

1. ¿De dónde es el señor Pérez? (Inglaterra)

   _____

2. ¿De dónde soy yo? (Estados Unidos) yo → answer with tú

   _____

3. ¿De dónde sois vosotros? (Italia) vosotros → answer with nosotros

   _____

4. ¿De dónde son Elena y Julio? (Canadá)

   _____

5. ¿De dónde somos nosotros? (España) nosotros → answer with vosotros

   _____

6. ¿De dónde es Martín? (Alemania)

   _____

7. ¿De dónde son ellos? (Bélgica)

   _____

8. ¿De dónde eres tú? (Brasil)

   _____

15.3 Giving and following directions

Everyone needs to know how to follow directions while traveling. Therefore, it's essential to understand them in Spanish when you're in a Spanish speaking country. Some verbs you'll need to know are:

English	Spanish	Pronunciation
to take	**tomar**	*[toh-mahr]*
to continue	**seguir**	*[seh-geer]*
to drive forward	**avanzar**	*[ah-bahn-thahr]*
to turn	**doblar**	*[doh-blahr]*
to make a turn	**girar**	*[hee-rahr]*
to explain	**explicar**	*[ehks-plee-kahr]*
to reach	**llegar**	*[yeh-gahr]*

Speak Abroad
Academy

Adverbs of Time

⮀ después (*after*)

⮀ luego (*after, then*)

⮀ entonces (*then*)

⮀ mientras (*meanwhile/meantime*)

Vocabulary: The Street

English	Spanish	Pronunciation
the block	**la cuadra**	*[lah kwah-drah]*
the street	**la calle**	*[lah kah-yeh]*
the avenue	**la avenida**	*[lah ah-beh-nee-dah]*
the sidewalk	**la acera**	*[lah ah-theh-rah]*
the main square	**la plaza principal**	*[lah plah-thah preen-thee-pahl]*
the traffic light	**el semáforo**	*[ehl seh-mah-foh-roh]*
straight	**derecho**	*[deh-reh-choh]*
the train tracks	**las vías del tren**	*[lahs beeh-as dehl trehn]*
to the right	**a la derecha**	*[ah lah deh-reh-chah]*
to the left	**a la izquierda**	*[ah lah eeth-kyehr-dah]*
the corner	**la esquina**	*[lah ehs-kee-nah]*
the bus stop	**la parada de ómnibus**	*[lah pah-rah-dah deh om-nih-buhs]*
north	**norte**	*[nohr-teh]*
south	**sur**	*[soor]*
west	**oeste**	*[oh-ehs-teh]*
east	**este**	*[ehs-teh]*
the intersection	**la intersección**	*[lah een-tehr-sehk-thyohn]*
the traffic circle	**la rotonda**	*[lah rroh-tohn-dah]*
the police	**el policía**	*[ehl poh-lee-thee-ah]*
the officer	**el agente**	*[ehl ah-hehn-teh]*

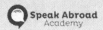

Time for words! Let's practice a bit!

15.3. Practice

A. You're in a Spanish-speaking city. How would you ask for these directions? **Example: Excuse me, could you please tell me where there is a public bathroom? <u>Disculpe, ¿puede decirme por favor dónde hay un baño público?</u>**

1. Please, can you tell me where the closest restaurant is?
    Por favor, ¿puede decirme _____?

2. Excuse me, can you tell me how many blocks there are to the supermarket?
    Disculpe, ¿puede decirme _____?

3. Could you please tell me how to get to the main square?
    Por favor, ¿puede decirme _____?

4. Excuse me, can you please tell me where the drugstore is?
    Disculpe, puede decirme por favor_____?

5. Could you please tell me where the bus stop is?
    Por favor, ¿puede decirme _____?

B. Now see if you can translate the dialogue below.

En la calle

TERESA: Buenos días, ¿sabe dónde está el banco?

AGENTE: Sí, le explico. Es hacia el norte. Debe seguir por esta avenida hasta llegar a la intersección. Luego, debe doblar a la derecha y avanzar hasta el semáforo, hacia el este.

TERESA: ¿Cuántas cuadras son hasta el semáforo?

AGENTE: Son cinco cuadras hasta el semáforo. En el semáforo, debe doblar a la izquierda, hacia el norte, y seguir dos cuadras. Llega a una rotonda. La rodea y continúa por la misma calle una cuadra. Luego debe girar a la derecha y avanzar siete cuadras más. Luego dobla de nuevo a la izquierda y avanza una cuadra más. El banco está en la esquina, a la derecha.

TERESA: Muchas gracias, agente. ¡Espero llegar!

C. You're in a Spanish speaking country and you want to help a lost tourist by giving them directions. Translate the following suggestions to Spanish. **Example: You should turn left at the light → <u>Debe doblar a la izquierda en el semáforo.</u>**

1. You should continue on the avenue until you get to the corner.
2. You should turn right and continue straight.
3. You should continue straight until you reach the light.
4. You should make a turn at the light.
5. You should turn left and continue five blocks until you get to the main square.
6. You should drive forward until you get to the intersection.

ANSWER KEY

CHAPTER 1: SUBJECT PRONOUNS

PRACTICE 1.1

A	1. nosotras	2. yo	3. ellas	4. ellos	5. vosotros	6. tú	7. ustedes	8. nosotros
B	1. yo	2. nosotros	3. vosotros	4. ustedes	5. ellos	6. tú		
C	1. él y ella	2. ellos	3. vosotros	4. vosotros	5. nosotros/ ellos	6. él	7. ella	

PRACTICE 1.2

A	1. usted	2. tú	3. usted	4. usted	5. tú	6. usted	7. usted	8. tú	9. tú	10. usted
B	1. ustedes	2. vosotros	3. ustedes	4. vosotros	5. ustedes	6. tú				

PRACTICE 1.3

A	1. c	2. d	3. e	4. g	5. f	6. a	7. b
B	1. Buenas tardes	2. Buenos días	3. Buenas noches	4. Buenas noches	5. Buenos días		
C	1. Disculpe / Perdón	2. Permiso	3. No es nada	4. Permiso	5. Disculpe	6. De nada	
D	1. De nada	2. Bien, ¿y tú?	3. Muy bien, gracias	4. Hasta luego	5. No es nada		
E	1. ¿Qué tal?	2. ¿y tú?	3. bien	4. Hasta	5. Adiós		

CHAPTER 2: NOUNS AND ARTICLES

PRACTICE 2.1

1. la	2. el	3. la	4. la	5. el	6. la	7. la	8. el	9. el	10. el
11. el	12. el	13. el	14. el	15. el	16. la	17. el	18. la	19. la	20. el

PRACTICE 2.2

A	1. los hombres	2. las amigas	3. las conversaciones	4. los animales	5. los sistemas	6. los niños	7. las casas	8. los trenes	9. las ciudades	10. los doctores
B	1. la verdad	2. la televisión	3. la mano	4. la perra	5. el lápiz	6. la niña	7. la radio	8. la comida		

PRACTICE 2.3

A	1. unos abuelos	2. unas conversaciones	3. unos perros	4. unas mujeres	5. unos estudiantes
	6. unos doctores	7. unos hoteles	8. unos trenes	9. unos lápices	10. unas ciudades
B	1. los estudiantes	2. los planetas	3. una doctora	4. unas fotos	5. el idioma
	6. los turistas	7. unos amigos	8. un tomate	9. la conversación	10. unas verdades
C	1. la	2. una	3. la / un	4. una	5. unas
	6. el	7. un	8. las		
D	1. the book	2. the house	3. the flowers	4. the youngster	5. the brothers
	6. the coffee	7. the train	8. the planets	9. a cat	10. some dogs
	11. the telephone	12. the hands	13. a program	14. some systems	15. the books
	16. the city				
E	1. la	2. unos	3. una	4. el	5. una
	6. las	7. el	8. un	9. las	
F	1. una	2. la	3. la	4. la	5. el
	6. una	7. las	8. un		

CHAPTER 3: DESCRIBING PEOPLE AND THINGS

PRACTICE 3.1

A	1. alta	2. pobre	3. fiel	4. hermosa	5. difícil
	6. bueno	7. feliz	8. interesante	9. fuerte	10. débil
B	1. baja	2. excelente	3. pequeña	4. simpático	5. viejo
	6. malo	7. inteligente	8. fiel	9. trabajador	10. gordo
C	1. El tema difícil	2. El niño alto	3. El restaurante bueno	4. La niña simpática	5. El perro grande
	6. El hombre débil				
D	1. los tomates grandes	2. los hombres altos	3. los perros inteligentes	4. las niñas fuertes	5. las personas trabajadoras
	6. las ciudades pequeñas	7. los gatos flacos	8. las mujeres alegres	9. los libros difíciles	10. las comidas excelentes
E	1. excelentes	2. trabajadora	3. hermosa	4. pequeños	5. hermosos
	6. buenas	7. gordos	8. simpáticos		

PRACTICE 3.2

1. norteamericana	2. francesa	3. inglés	4. italiana	5. español	6. alemana

Speak Abroad
Academy

PRACTICE 3.3

A	1. inteligente - hermosa	2. alegre - interesante	3. grande - interesante	4. bueno - simpático	5. malos - blancos	6. simpáticos - alegres
B	1. gordo, grande, hermoso, bueno, interesante, simpático	2. limpia, interesante, trabajadora	3. gordo, interesante, simpático, hermoso, bueno, grande	4. interesante, grande, simpático, gordo, bueno, hermoso	5. grande, simpático, gordo, bueno, interesante, hermoso	6. grande, limpia, interesante
C	1. francesa	2. italiano	3. alemán	4. española	5. portuguesa	6. inglés
D	1. español	2. francés	3. inglés	4. italiano	5. español	6. norteamericana

CHAPTER 4: DESCRIBING THINGS

PRACTICE 4.1

A	1. feliz, marrón, fiel, inteligente, vieja	2. nuevo, marrón	3. inteligente, trabajadora, interesante, feliz, fiel	4. rápido, nuevo, marrón	5. interesante, moreno, rápido, feliz, inteligente, fiel, alto, rico	6. cara, vieja, nueva, barata, marrón
	7. nuevo, rico, sabroso, marrón	8. trabajadora, interesante, feliz, inteligente, vieja, fiel, anciana	9. cara, vieja, nueva, barata	10. trabajadora, interesante, feliz, inteligente, vieja, fiel, anciana	11. interesante, difícil, nuevo, fácil	12. trabajadora, interesante, feliz, inteligente
	13. interesante, difícil, rápido, nuevo, fácil	14. interesante, moreno, rápido, feliz, inteligente, fiel, alto, rico	15. cara, interesante, vieja, nueva, barata, marrón	16. cara, vieja, nueva, barata, marrón	17. interesante, difícil, fácil	18. nuevo, rico, sabroso
B	1. amarilla	2. azul	3. anaranjada, naranja		4. blanca	5. negra
	6. gris	7. verde	8. Rosado, rosa		9. marrón	10. rojo
C	1. También es amable.		2. También es fácil.		3. También son trabajadores.	
	4. También son gordos.		5. También es buena		6. También son fuertes.	
D	1. alta, trabajadora, rubia, feliz y rica		2. grande, fea, vieja, cara y baja		3. pobre, poco inteligente, moreno, bajo, perezoso y joven	

PRACTICE 4.2

A	1. Esta camisa es linda.	2. Estos zapatos son caros.	3. Este suéter es de lana.	4. Estos vestidos son de seda.	5. Estos pantalones son baratos.
B	1. Esa blusa es blanca.	2. Esa camiseta es roja.	3. Esas faldas son cortas.	4. Esa chaqueta es muy barata.	5. Esas zapatillas deportivas son hermosas.
C	1. ¿Quién es ese doctor? Este doctor es un cardiólogo.	2. Este planeta es muy grande.	3. Aquella casa es hermosa.	4. Aquel tren es grande.	5. Esa moto es nueva.
	6. Ese joven es simpático.	7. El estudiante es aquel muchacho.			

D	1. ¿Es feliz esta niña? No, es infeliz.	2. ¿Son ricos estos muchachos? No, son pobres.	3. ¿Es feo este perro? No, es lindo.	4. ¿Son viejos estos edificios? No, son nuevos.	5. ¿Es anciana esta mujer? No, es joven.
	6. ¿Son fuertes estas muchachas? No, son débiles.	7. ¿Es grande esta casa? No, es pequeña.	8. ¿Es alto este niño? No, es bajo.		

PRACTICE 4.3

A	1. Aquella casa es muy grande.	2. Aquel edificio es el correo y aquel árbol es muy viejo.	3. Aquella calle es nueva y aquellos perros son malos.	4. Aquella avenida es ancha.		
B	1. Este sistema es excelente.	2. Estas pescaderías son caras.	3. Esta ciudad es hermosa.	4. Este teatro es pequeño.	5. Esas oficinas son nuevas.	6. Esos coches son amarillos.

CHAPTER 5: THE VERB SER (TO BE)

PRACTICE 5

A	1. Luis es de Estados Unidos.	2. Tomás es de Francia.	3. Están en Madrid.	4. Son turistas.	5. La señora es de Madrid.	
B	1. Luciano Pavarotti es de Italia. Es italiano.	2. Frida Kahlo es de México. Es mexicana.	3. Johnny Depp es de Estados Unidos. Es estadounidense.	4. Albert Einstein es de Alemania. Es alemán.	5. Coco Chanel es de Francia. Es francesa.	6. Rafael Nadal es de España. Es español.
	7. Cristiano Ronaldo es de Portugal. Es portugués.	8. Paul McCartney es de Inglaterra. Es inglés.				
C	1. Mick Jagger es inglés (identification).	2. Las sillas son de plástico (material something is made of).	3. Nosotros somos de Colombia (origin).	4. Las mesas son de madera (material something is made of).	5. La comida es para la niña (for whom something is intended).	6. Es lunes (day of the week).
	7. Marcos y Luis son abogados (profession).	8. La fiesta es en el club (where an event takes place).	9. El perro es de María (possession).	10. El libro es amarillo (description).	11. Es el 14 de febrero (date).	
D	1. Es de plástico o de vidrio	2. Es de madera o de plástico	3. Es de ladrillos	4. Son de cuero	5. Son de vidrio	6. Es de madera
	7. Es de metal	8. Es de papel				
E	1. es	2. son	3. es	4. son	5. son	6. es
F	1. Ellos son de Alemania	2. Tú y Alejandra sois/son de Argentina.	3. Vosotros sois de Colombia.	4. Nosotros somos de México.	5. Yo soy de Francia.	6. Felipe es de Brasil.
G	1. es	2. soy	3. somos	4. es	5. son	6. eres
	7. sois	8. es	9. sois/son			
H	1. son las tres de la tarde	2. es el primero de mayo	3. es el 3 de noviembre	4. es miércoles	5. son las diez de la mañana	6. es domingo

I	1. Sí, soy simpático	2. Sí, somos estudiantes	3. No, no es pequeña la casa de Mariana (or Sí, es pequeña la casa de Mariana)	4. Elena es de Inglaterra	5. Es importante estudiar	6. Son las 4:00 p.m.
J	1. Los perros son del niño	2. El libro es del colegio	3. Aquella casa es del hombre rico	4. La moto es del joven	5. La comida es del restaurante	6. El coche es del muchacho

CHAPTER 6: ESTAR (TO BE) AND TENER (TO HAVE)

PRACTICE 6.1

A	1. París y Lyon están en Francia. (location)	2. La niña está enferma. (health)	3. Está triste. (changing mood)	4. Juan está delgado (changing condition)	5. Nosotros estamos aquí. (location)	6. La comida está deliciosa. (personal opinion)
	7. Vosotros estáis contentos. (changing mood)	8. Tú estás cansada. (changing condition)				

B	1. La mesa y las sillas están sucias.	2. Él es abogado.	3. Nosotros estamos cansados.	4. Es importante estudiar.	5. Vosotros estáis en la universidad.	6. Martín y Luis son inteligentes.
	7. El café es para la mujer.	8. La ciudad es hermosa.	9. Tú eres una turista.	10. Yo soy de Guatemala.	11. La lección es fácil.	12. El niño está en el colegio.
	13. Ustedes están contentos.	14. Nosotros somos italianos.	15. Sara está triste.			

C	1. Tim es español.	2. El restaurante está cerrado.	3. Las hijas de Pedro son rubias e inteligentes.	4. El problema es muy fácil.	5. El libro es interesante.	6. Tú estás furioso.
	7. La banana es amarilla.	8. Nosotros estamos felices.	9. La foto está en la silla.			

D	1. es	2. es	3. está	4. están	5. está	6. está	7. es	8. está

E	1. X	2. X	3. X	4. ✓	5. X	6. X	7. ✓	8. X	9. X	10. ✓	11. X

F	1. Teresa y Miguel están en el cine	2. Vosotros estáis enfermos	3. La universidad es buena	4. CORRECT	5. Tú eres buena abogada	6. Yo soy de Perú
	7. CORRECT	8. Las sillas son de plástico	9. Susana es inteligente	10. CORRECT	11. La moto es de Federico	12. Hoy es miércoles

PRACTICE 6.2

A	1. tenemos		2. tienen		3. tenéis/tienen	4. tiene		5. tengo	
	6. tiene		7. tiene		8. tenemos	9. tienes		10. tiene	
B	1. tienen	2. tengo	3. tienes		4. tenemos	5. tenéis	6. tiene	7. tiene	8. Tienen
C	1. X	2. X	3. ✓	4. ✓	5. X	6. X	7. X	8. X	

D	1. Nosotros tenemos sesenta años.	2. Ustedes tienen cuarenta años.	3. CORRECT	4. CORRECT	5. Tú tienes quince años.
	6. María tiene seis años.	7. Tú y Miguel tenéis/ tienen setenta años.	8. Josefina tiene veintitrés años.		
E	1. tengo	2. tenemos	3. tiene	4. tienes	5. tenéis
	6. tiene	7. tienen	8. tiene	9. tiene	

CHAPTER 7: NUMBERS

PRACTICE 7.1

1. un	2. un	3. una	4. uno	5. un	6. una

PRACTICE 7.2

A	1. X Hay una alfombra en la casa.	2. X Hay tigres en el zoológico.	3. ✓	4. ✓	5. X Hay oficinas en el edificio.
	6. ✓	7. X Hay turistas en la ciudad.	8. X Hay personas en el cine.		
B	1. Are there flowers in the garden?	2. Are there chairs in the office?	3. Are there cats in the street?	4. Are there hotels in the city?	5. Is there a television in the house?
	6. Are there doctors in the hospital?	7. Is there a dog in the car?	8. Is there a radio in the car?	9. Are there two women in the fish store?	10. Are there tables in a restaurant?
C	1. No hay animales en el zoológico.	2. No hay muchos niños en el parque.	3. No hay un teléfono público en la calle.	4. No hay mucha gente en el restaurante.	5. No hay un buen hotel en la ciudad.
	6. No hay muchos planetas en el cielo.				

D	1. está	2. hay	3. está	4. está	5. hay	6. hay	7. hay	8. está	9. está	10. hay

PRACTICE 7.3

A	1. hace calor	2. hace frío	3. hay viento/ está ventoso/ ventea	4. hace sol	5. está lloviendo/ hay lluvia/ llueve
	6. hay nieve/ está nevando/ nieva	7. está nublado/ hay nubes			
B	1. hacemos	2. hacen	3. hago	4. hacen	5. hace
	6. hace	7. haces	8. hacéis	9. hace	

PRACTICE 7.4

A	1. cuántos	2. cuánta	3. cuántos	4. cuántas	5. cuántos	6. cuánto
B	1. Hay siete días en una semana.	2. Hay cuatro semanas en un mes.	3. Hay 365 días en un año.	4. Hay dos días en un fin de semana.	5. Hay veintiocho días en el mes de febrero.	6. Hay cinco dedos en mi mano.
	7. Hay dos (number varies) hospitales en mi ciudad.	8. Hay una (number varies) televisión en mi casa.	9. Hay tres (number varies) árboles en mi jardín.	10. Hay veinte (number varies) sillas en mi casa.		
C	1. Hay dos universidades en la ciudad.	2. Hay veinte manzanas en la canasta.	3. Hay doce meses en el año.	4. Hay una estatua de la Libertad en Nueva York.	5. Hay dos ojos en la cara.	6. Hay muchos edificios en la ciudad.

CHAPTER 8: SABER AND CONOCER

PRACTICE 8.1

1. sabemos	2. sabes	3. sabéis	4. sabe	5. sé	6. sabe	7. saben	8. sabe

PRACTICE 8.2

A	1. conocen	2. conoce	3. conocéis	4. conocemos	5. conozco	6. conoce	7. conoces	8. conoce
B	1. conoce	2. sabéis	3. saben	4. sabe	5. conoce	6. conoces	7. sé	8. conocen/ conocéis
C	1. conozco	2.sabemos	3. conocéis	4. conoce	5. sabes	6. saben	7. conozco	8. conoce
	9. saben							
D	1. X	2. a	3. X	4. X	5. a	6. a	7. a	

PRACTICE 8.3

A	1. Novak Djokovic sabe jugar al tenis	2. LeBron James sabe jugar al baloncesto.	3. Tiger Woods sabe jugar al golf.	4. J. K. Rowling sabe escribir novelas.	5. Lionel Messi y Cristiano Ronaldo saben jugar al fútbol.
	6. Taylor Swift sabe cantar.	7. Michael Phelps sabe nadar.	8. Shakira sabe bailar.	9. Meryl Streep sabe actuar.	10. Simon Biles sabe hacer gimnasia artística.
B	1. Sherlock Holmes conoce a Watson.	2. Ashton Kutcher conoce a Mila Kunis.	3. Rhett Butler conoce a Scarlett O'Hara.	4. Chris Martin conoce a Dakota Johnson.	5. David Beckham conoce a Victoria Beckham.
	6. Adán conoce a Eva.	7. Justin Bieber conoce a Hailey Bieber.			

C	1. Yo conozco al profesor Blanco.	2. Mi hermana y yo conocemos a la madre de Juan.	3. María y Luis conocen a Sergio.	4. Vosotros conocéis al director del área comercial.	5. Tú conoces a la tía Julia.
	6. Carlos conoce a la tía Julia.	7. Martín y Elena conocen a la tía Julia.			

D	1. Yo sé la verdad.	2. Ella conoce a María.	3. Ellos saben nadar.	4. Pedro y Elena conocen Nueva York.	5. Sabemos la respuesta.	6. Conocemos al estudiante.
	7. Tú sabes mi nombre.		8. Él sabe la verdad.	9. El perro conoce a Juan.	10. Sé tocar el piano.	11. Conocemos la universidad.

E	1. sabe	2. conozco	3. conoces	4. saben	5. conoce

CHAPTER 9: THE INDICATIVE MOOD: PRESENT TENSE OF HABLAR, COMER, VIVIR

PRACTICE 9.1

A	At the Grocer's	
	LUISA:	Good morning, do you have bananas?
	GROCER:	Good morning. Yes, I do have bananas.
	LUISA:	Oh, how much are they?
	GROCER:	They are 20 pesos for a kilogram.
	LUISA:	Very well. I need to buy two kilograms.
	GROCER:	Ok. Here you are.
	LUISA:	Thank you very much. Goodbye.

B	1. yo	2. nosotros	3. ustedes / ellos	4. él/ ella/ usted	5. yo
	6. tú	7. él/ ella/ usted	8. vosotros	9. ellos/ ellas/ ustedes	10. tú

C	1. falso	2. falso	3. cierto	4. falso

D	1. trabaja	2. miran	3. buscáis	4. enseña	5. compro
	6. viajan	7. explicamos	8. arregla		

E

Infinitive	hablar	enseñar	trabajar	mirar
yo	hablo	enseño	trabajo	miro
tú	hablas	enseñas	trabajas	miras
él/ella/usted	habla	enseña	trabaja	mira
nosotros	hablamos	enseñamos	trabajamos	miramos
vosotros	habláis	enseñáis	trabajáis	miráis
ellas/ellos/ ustedes	hablan	enseñan	trabajan	miran

PRACTICE 9.2

A	1. No, son quince personas en la mesa.	2. Sí, todos trabajan en la misma oficina.	3. Sí, tienen pollo y pescado.	4. No, tienen una mesa grande.				
B	1. comprende	2. prenden	3. corre	4. vendemos	5. coméis	6. bebemos	7. leo	8. aprendes

C

Infinitive	comer	vender	creer	apender
yo	como	vendo	creo	aprendo
tú	comes	vendes	crees	aprendes
él/ella/usted	come	vende	cree	aprende
nosotros	comemos	vendemos	creemos	aprendemos
vosotros	coméis	vendéis	creéis	aprendéis
ellas/ellos/ustedes	comen	venden	creen	aprenden

PRACTICE 9.3

A	1. comparten	2. suben	3. vive... vive	4. abro	5. recibes	6. escribís	7. discutimos	8. decides

B

Infinitive	escribir	recibir	abrir	subir
yo	escribo	recibo	abro	subo
tú	escribes	recibes	abres	subes
él/ella/usted	escribe	recibe	abre	sube
nosotros	escribimos	recibimos	abrimos	subimos
vosotros	escribís	recibís	abrís	subís
ellas/ellos/ustedes	escriben	reciben	abren	suben

CHAPTER 10: WHAT TIME IS IT?

PRACTICE 10.1

A	1. Son las nueve y diez	2. Son las seis y cinco	3. Son las siete y veinticinco	4. Son las doce y cuarto		
B	1. Son las cuatro menos cuarto	2. Son las once en punto	3. Es la una y media	4. Son las siete menos cuarto	5. Son las ocho y cuarto	6. Son las nueve y veinte
C	1. Son las ocho. Es hora de trabajar.	2. Son las diez. Es hora de caminar.	3. Es la una y cuarto. Es hora de comer.	4. Son las cuatro y media. Es hora de regresar a casa.	5. Son las seis. Es hora de buscar a mis hijos.	6. Son las ocho. Es hora de cenar.
D	1. ¿A qué hora viajamos a París? A las doce en punto.	2. ¿A qué hora viajamos a Madrid? A la una en punto.	3. ¿A qué hora viajamos a Praga? A las cinco y media.	4. ¿A qué hora viajamos a Lima? A las nueve y cuarto.	5. ¿A qué hora viajamos a Buenos Aires? A las nueve menos cuarto.	6. ¿A qué hora viajamos a Washington? A las seis menos cuarto.

PRACTICE 10.2

A	1.Es a las doce del mediodía.	2. Es a las cuatro de la tarde.	3. Es a las ocho de la mañana.	4. Es a las once de la mañana.	5. Es a las doce de la medianoche.	6. Es a las tres de la tarde.
B	1. Son las once en punto.	2. Son las ocho y media.	3. Son las ocho de la mañana.	4. Son las tres de la tarde más o menos.	5. Son las diez y media.	6. Son las cinco y media.
	7. Son las siete y veinte.	8. Es la una menos veinte./ Veinte para la una.	9. Son las dos menos cinco./ Cinco para las dos.	10. Son las dos menos veinticinco./ Veinticinco para las dos.	11. Son las ocho y cuarto.	12. Son las cuatro menos cuarto./ Cuarto para las cuatro.

PRACTICE 10.3

A	1. El lunes es gris.	2. El lunes es triste.	3. La gente vive en soledad.	4. No saben mirar.		
B	1. A las cuatro y cuarto	2. A las nueve y cuarto	3. A las diez y media	4. De lunes a viernes	5. Los sábados	6. Los domingos

PRACTICE 10.4

A	1.Mi cumpleaños es el (answer varies)	2. La independencia de Estados Unidos se celebra el cuatro de julio.	3. El verano empieza el 21 de junio en Europa.	4. Navidad es el 25 de diciembre.	5. Año Nuevo es el primero de enero.	
B	1. Flores → primavera. En primavera hay flores.	2. Sol → verano. En verano hay sol.	3. Hojas secas → otoño. En otoño hay hojas secas.	4. Calor → verano. En verano hace calor.	5. Viento → otoño. En otoño hay viento.	6. Hielo → invierno. En invierno hay hielo.

Answer key

Speak Abroad
Academy

CHAPTER 11: AFFIRMATIVE AND NEGATIVE SENTENCES

PRACTICE 11

A	1. No, Teresa no desea comer nada.	2. No, Teresa no desea beber nada.	3. No, Teresa no desea nada.	4. No, Teresa nunca cena por la noche.	
B	1. nada	2. nadie	3. ninguno	4. nunca	5. tampoco
	6. algo	7. alguien	8. alguno	9. siempre	10. también
C	1. ¿Tienes alguna fruta?	2. ¿Tienes algún suéter?	3. No tengo ninguna camisa.	4. ¿Compraste alguna blusa?	5. No, no compré ninguna blusa.
	6. ¿Hay algunos niños en la piscina?	7. No, no hay ningún niño en la piscina.	8. ¿Tienes algún gato en casa?	9. No, no tengo ningún gato en casa.	10. ¿Tienen alguna maleta en el coche?
	11. No, no tengo ninguna maleta en el coche.				
D	1. No, no hay nada.	2. Sí, hay algo (the banana).	3. No, no hay nada.	4. Sí, hay algo (his wallet).	5. No, no hay nada.	6. Sí, hay algo (his keys).
E	Answers vary. If there is someone "Sí, hay alguien". If there is no one, "No, no hay nadie" is correct.
F	1. Sí, hay algunas. No, no hay ninguna.	2. Sí, hay algunos. No, no hay ninguno.	3. Sí, hay algunos. No, no hay ninguno.	4. Sí, hay algunas. No, no hay ninguna.	5. Sí, hay algunas. No, no hay ninguna.
	6. Sí, hay algunos. No, no hay ninguno.				
G	1. No hay nada delicioso en la cocina.	2. No tengo ninguna flor en mi jardín.	3. Maria no estudia allí tampoco.	4. Sofía no estudia nunca la lección.	5. No meten nada en el coche.
	6. No reciben nunca a sus amigos.	7. No venden bananas en esa verdulería tampoco.			
H	1. nunca... nada	2. jamás	3. ni... ni	4. nada	5. nadie
	6. tampoco	7. ningún	8. ninguna		
I	1. No, no compartimos nada.	2. No, Tomás no recibe nada por su cumpleaños.	3. No, no hay ningún restaurante en esta calle.	4. No, no canto nunca.	5. No, ellos no trabajaron nada por la mañana.
	6. No, no leen ningún periódico los domingos.	7. No, no hay ninguna flor en el invierno.	8. No, nunca voy al supermercado los sábados.	9. No, los turistas no visitan ningún parque.	10. No, vosotros no coméis nada de carne.
J	1. Nunca está triste.	2. Nosotros no hacemos nada de deporte hoy.	3. María no necesita comprar libros tampoco.	4. Este supermercado no es nada pequeño.	5. Nadie estudia en la biblioteca.
	6. Ninguna niña baila en el colegio.	7. No, no hay ninguna verdulería aquí.	8. Martín no bebe agua (or Martín no bebe nada).	9. Vosotros nunca limpiáis la casa (or Vosotros nunca limpiáis nada).	10. Yo no conozco a ninguno de sus amigos (or Yo no conozco a ningún amigo de él).

CHAPTER 12: CONJUNCTIONS AND INDEFINITE ADJECTIVES

PRACTICE 12.1

A	1. María e Inés	2. Hay diez u once niños	3. Toma la llave e intenta abrir la puerta.	4. Él nos llama e invita.	5. Vió algo u oyó un ruido.	6. (Ella) Sabe leer y escribir muy bien.
B	1. y	2. o	3. pero	4. o	5. y	6. pero	7. o	8. pero
C	1. pero	2. sino	3. pero	4. sin embargo	5. aunque	6. aunque
D	1. porque	2. pero	3. aunque	4. Ni... ni	5. e	6. Tanto... como
	7. y	8. aunque				

PRACTICE 12.2

A	1. Pedro y Luis no saben si sus amigos regresan hoy.	2. Mirta pregunta si hay examen mañana.	3. José decide si sube el Monte Fitz Roy.	4. Vosotros no sabéis si Paula necesita algo para la fiesta.	5. Usted pregunta si los empleados trabajan bien.	6. Tú decides si bebes café o té.
B	1. Ella sabe que vivimos en la calle Oro.	2. Juan piensa que viajamos todo el año.	3. Yo creo que el señor Ortiz arregla hornos.	4. Juana dice que a José le gusta comer.	5. La profesora nos dice que es tarde.	6. La madre dice que los niños necesitan lápices nuevos.
C	1. Me gusta que mis hijos ordenan solos.	2. Trabajo mucho pero gano poco.	3. Aunque hace frío, hay sol.	4. Martín cree que está demasiado ventoso para correr.	5. El verdulero me explica que los tomates están verdes.	6. Llegas temprano porque sales temprano.

PRACTICE 12.3

A	1. muchas	2. tantos	3. mismo	4. otra	5. algunas	6. cada	7. otras	8. toda
B	1. She has many dogs and cats.	2. Maria has several daughters, but she has no sons.	3. Both Luis and Juan have few friends.	4. She/he neither reads magazines nor newspapers.	5. She/he knows other countries since she/he travels a lot.		
	6. She/he has the same car as Laura.	7. She/he knows every street in Paris, but she/he doesn't know her/his own city.	8. She/he speaks some languages, but she/he doesn't speak English.	9. It's the same friendship, though we're older.	10. All languages are useful, even if some are more useful than others.		
C	1. Ningún día es hermoso.	2. Tengo muchas tristezas.	3. Hay tan pocas cosas lindas en la vida.	4. Tengo pocos amigos.	5. Todos los días son malos.	6. Toda tarea es imposible.

Answer key

Speak Abroad
Academy

CHAPTER 13: LIKES AND DISLIKES

PRACTICE 13.1

A	1. nos	2. os	3. les	4. les	5. les	6. me	7. te	8. le	9. le

B						
	1. A mí me gusta el coche.	2. A ellos les gustan las cebollas.	3. A nosotros no nos gusta leer.	4. A ti te gustan las bananas.	5. A vosotros os gusta trabajar.	6. A Marcos le gusta estudiar.
	7. A Elsa le gustan los tomates.	8. A mi padre le gusta comer.	9. A mi madre le gusta el pescado.	10. A los chicos no les gusta la leche.	11. A María le gusta el pollo.	

C						
	1. A nosotros nos gusta correr.	2. A los niños no les gustan las verduras.	3. A mí me gustan esos zapatos.	4. A Luis y Teresa les gustan las fiestas.	5. A Elena le gusta tocar piano.	6. A mí me gusta el pescado.

D						
	(Answers may vary) 1. No me gusta Cristiano Ronaldo, aunque me gusta Leo Messi.	2. No me gusta comer pastas, pero me gusta comer hamburguesas.	3. No me gusta el café; sin embargo, me gusta el té.	4. No me gusta la actriz (actress) Judy Dench, pero me gusta la actriz Meryl Streep.	5. No me gusta el tenista Medvedev, aunque me gusta el tenista Federer.	6. No me gusta estudiar en el comedor, pero me gusta estudiar en la biblioteca.
	7. No me gustan los gatos, pero me gustan los perros.	8. No me gusta viajar en tren; sin embargo, me gusta viajar en coche.				

E	1. les gustan	2. os gustan	3. te gustan	4. nos gusta	5. me gustan	6. le gustan

F						
	1. ¿A nosotros nos gustan las fiestas?	2. ¿A Teresa le gusta su universidad?	3. ¿A ellos les gusta recibir gente en su casa?	4. ¿A mí me gusta hacer yoga?	5. ¿A ti te gusta el pescado?	6. ¿A usted le gusta viajar?

G						
	1. A nosotros nos gusta trabajar.	2. A ustedes les gusta vivir solos.	3. A vosotros os gusta caminar en el parque los sábados.	4. A Carolina y Luis les gusta subir montañas.	5. A ti te gusta invitar amigos a tu casa.	6. A ellos les gusta viajar por el mundo.

H						
	1. A mí me gustan los caramelos.	2. A ti te gusta el pan.	3. A vosotros os gusta la leche.	4. A ti te gusta el café.	5. A ellos les gustan las naranjas.	6. A él le gusta la carne.

I						
	1. Al abuelo le gusta cocinar.	2. Al hermano le gusta hacer surf.	3. A la tía le gusta leer libros.	4. A los primos les gusta comprar ropa.	5. Al padre le gusta comer y beber.	6. A la hija le gusta buscar caracoles en la orilla.
	7. A la madre le gusta la tranquilidad.	8. A los sobrinos les gusta correr por la playa.				

PRACTICE 13.2

1. Me gustaría un vaso de agua.	2. Quiero dormir.	3. Me gustaría hablar bien el español.	4. Me gustaría ese vestido verde.	5. Quiero arreglar el techo.

CHAPTER 14: PREPOSITIONS I

PRACTICE 14.1

A	1. en	2. con	3. de	4. de	5. con	6. en	7. de	8. con	9. en
B	1. de... de	2. con	3. de	4. en	5. con	6. con			
C	1. en	2. en	3. entre	4. entre	5. entre	6. en			

PRACTICE 14.2

A	1. para	2. sin	3. a	4. para	5. a	6. sin	7. a	8. sin
B	1. a	2. X	3. a	4. X	5. X	6. a		
C	1. a... a	2. a	3. de... de	4. de	5. de	6. a	7. de	8. de
D	1. de	2. desde	3. de	4. desde	5. desde	6. desde		

PRACTICE 14.3

A	1. por	2. para	3. según	4. hasta/por	5. por	6. contra
	7. hasta	8. para	9. según			
B	1. hasta	2. según	3. para	4. contra	5. hasta	6. hasta
C	1. sin	2. con	3. para	4. según	5. hacia	6. sobre
	7. durante/por	8. sobre	9. entre	10. a		

CHAPTER 15: PREPOSITIONS II

PRACTICE 15.1

A	1. dentro de	2. fuera de	3. encima de	4. debajo de	5. junto a	6. lejos de
B	1. fuera de	2. delante de	3. lejos de	4. debajo de	5. lejos de	
C	1. El coche está detrás del camión.	2. La cartera está dentro de la bolsa.	3. La silla está delante de la mesa.	4. La mochila está encima de la cama.	5. El gato está fuera de la casa.	6. El perro descansa bajo el puente.
D	1. El correo está junto al edificio municipal.	2. El cine está detrás del correo.	3. El supermercado está lejos de la plaza.	4. El bar está junto a la plaza.	5. Encima del edificio municipal hay un reloj.	6. La iglesia está cerca del correo.
E	1. La silla está en frente del/frente al escritorio.	2. La computadora está encima del escritorio.	3. La planta está debajo del cuadro.	4. Los juguetes están dentro de la caja.	5. El oso de peluche está delante de la caja.	6. El coche rojo está junto al oso de peluche.
F	1. La mochila está lejos del librero.	2. El cuadro está cerca de la biblioteca.	3. Los lápices están dentro del portalápices.	4. El oso de peluche está fuera de la caja.	5. El mapa está sobre la pared.	6. La pelota está debajo del escritorio.

PRACTICE 15.2

1. Es de Inglaterra.	2. Eres de Estados Unidos.	3. Somos de Italia.	4. Son de Canadá.	5. Sois de España.
6. Es de Alemania.	7. Son de Bélgica.	8. Soy de Brasil.		

PRACTICE 15.3

A	1. Por favor, ¿puede decirme dónde está el restaurante más cercano?	2. Disculpe, ¿puede decirme cuántas cuadras hay hasta el supermercado?	3. Por favor, ¿puede decirme cómo llegar a la plaza principal?	4. Disculpe, ¿puede decirme por favor dónde está la farmacia?	5. Por favor, ¿puede decirme dónde está la parada del ómnibus?	
B	TERESA:	Good morning. Do you know where the bank is?				
	OFFICER:	Yes, let me explain. It's towards the north. You need to follow this avenue until you reach the intersection. Then, turn right and keep on going until you reach the light, towards the east.				
	TERESA:	How many blocks are there until the streetlight?				
	OFFICER:	It's five blocks until the streetlight. At the light, you should turn left, towards north, and continue two blocks. You'll reach a traffic circle. Drive around it and continue on the same road for a block. Then turn right and keep going straight for seven blocks. Then turn left again and go one more block. The bank will be on the corner to the right.				
	TERESA:	Thank you very much, officer. I hope I get there!				
C	1. Debe seguir por la avenida hasta llegar a la esquina.	2. Debe doblar a la derecha y seguir derecho.	3. Debe seguir derecho hasta llegar al semáforo.	4. Debe girar en el semáforo.	5. Debe doblar a la izquierda y seguir cinco cuadras hasta llegar a la plaza principal.	6. Debe avanzar hasta llegar a la intersección.

Made in United States
Orlando, FL
03 November 2024

53309201R00083